T0246974

Beyond Cop Cities

Joy James, Ebenezer Fitch Professor of the Humanities at Williams College, is a political philosopher who works with organizers. She is editor of *The Angela Y. Davis Reader; Imprisoned Intellectuals;* and co-editor of *The Black Feminist Reader*. James's recent books include: *In Pursuit of Revolutionary Love; New Bones Abolition: Captive Maternal Agency and the (After)Life of Erica Garner,* and *Contextualizing Angela Davis: The Agency and Identity of an Icon*. Her edited volumes with Pluto also include *ENGAGE: Indigenous, Black, Afro-Indigenous Futures*.

Beyond Cop Cities

Dismantling State and Corporate-Funded Armies and Prisons

Edited by Joy James

PLUTO  PRESS

First published 2024 by Pluto Press
New Wing, Somerset House, Strand, London WC2R 1LA
and Pluto Press, Inc.
1930 Village Center Circle, 3-834, Las Vegas, NV 89134

www.plutobooks.com

British Library Cataloguing in Publication Data
A catalogue record for this book is available from the British
Library

ISBN 978 0 7453 5048 6   Paperback
ISBN 978 0 7453 5050 9   PDF
ISBN 978 0 7453 5049 3   EPUB

This book is printed on paper suitable for recycling and made
from fully managed and sustained forest sources. Logging,
pulping and manufacturing processes are expected to conform to
the environmental standards of the country of origin.

Typeset by Stanford DTP Services, Northampton, England

Printed in the UK.

Contents

PART II

Acknowledgments

Thank you to: Kalonji Changa, I. B., N.T., Noel Hanrahan for their contributions to this book. Also, thanks to *Inquest; Logos: A Journal of Modern Society and Culture*; C. Flux Sing, Mon M., James Jones, and Kevin "Rashid" Johnson for permission to repost content and art. Changa's RSTV/Black Power Media (Reloaded) provided interviews edited for this text. *BayView* first printed Kevin "Rashid" Johnson's article on prison gangs in April 2024.

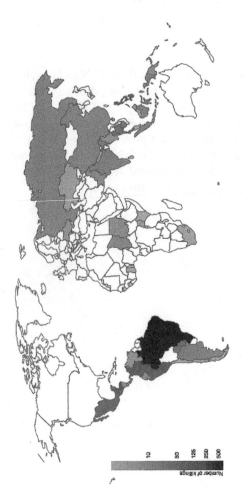

Global Killings of Land and Environmental Defenders 2002–14

(The Decolonial Atlas. https://decolonialatlas.wordpress.com/2015/06/08/murdered-environmentalists/)

Introduction

> The people, they won't leave
> What is threatenin' about divesting and wantin' peace?
> The problem isn't the protests, it's what they're protesting
> It goes against what our country is funding . . . .
> —Macklemore, "Hind's Hall," May 7, 2024*

Beyond Cop Cites: Dismantling State and Corporate-Funded Armies and Prisons critiques state violence and genocide embedded in U.S. domestic and foreign policies. It began as a zine pamphlet in August 2023, for political study and struggle around predatory policing, colonialism, anti-Black violence, and environmental defense. The zine was inspired by pamphlets such as *Beneath the Concrete, the Forest: Accounts from the Defense of the Atlanta Forest*, which was presented to me in March 2023, when I met with several Black "forest protectors" in Atlanta, Georgia.

The zine expanded into this book which includes articles first published in *Inquest* (Harvard Law), *Logos: A Journal of Modern Society and Culture* (Rutgers University), and interviews conducted by *Black Power Media* (founded by Kalonji Changa) podcasts "Guerrilla Intellectual University" and "Renegade Siafu TV" (RSTV). C. Flux Sing shared his art and generously offered to design

---

* Macklemore's "Hind's Hall" (www.instagram.com/macklemore/reel/C6o4830yMvE/) refers to Columbia University students occupying and renaming a campus building after Hind Rajab; Israeli Defense Forces (IDF) trapped and killed the six-year-old Gazan child and her family in their car in January 2024. For decades, the IDF has trained with U.S. police, sheriffs, border control, and FBI agents, according to Jewish Voice for Peace (www.jewishvoiceforpeace.org/2022/03/17/revealed-adl-us-israel-police-exchanges/#:~:text=Since+the+early+2000s%2C+thousands,Israeli+military+and+police+forces).

the book covers. The book includes a QR code/Omeka site that holds images, data, analyses gathered from the work of activists and intellectuals who oppose militarized and predatory policing and prisons (see page 112). This text also raises the important issues surrounding political prisoners and resistance to predatory policing, prisons and political repression.

In studying resistance to Cop Cities' expanding militaristic policing—and its entanglements with genocidal wars—contributors distinguish between "talking heads" from media and other sectors that sever radical resistance and engaged actors who align with the most vulnerable to policing and imprisonment: working class and economically impoverished Black, Indigenous and outcaste communities. Forest protectors include those who knew and loved "Tortuguita" killed in January 2023 by Georgia State Troopers, who were exonerated by city, state, federal governments.

Voter suppression tactics used by white nationalists (from post-reconstruction in the late 1800s to the early 1960s) were disabled by voting rights protections that have since been eviscerated by the ultra-conservative U.S. Supreme Court. Despite the sacrifices and deaths of civil rights activists seeking voter access for all decades ago, today Black elected and appointed officials deploy voter repression against the rights and needs of working-class Black communities. In the predominantly Black Atlanta City Council, the clerk voided signatures of thousands of voters.[1] Focused on conventional electoral politics, progressive leaders organized a referendum to collect signatures to block Atlanta's Cop City. That endeavor ended in predictable negative outcomes.[2] In August 2023, organizers to stop "Cop City" obtained 100k signatures for a referendum on the police training facility.[3] *The Intercept* reported that the Atlanta city government and its corporate donors, seeking to protect and expand Cop Cities, would circumvent democratic decision-making and block citizens seeking to preserve natural environments and curtail predatory policing.[4]

Astute organizers also anticipated and predicted that the referendum strategy, co-led by an Atlanta-based community nonprofit, reportedly with $2.3m in funding, would be derailed by the Atlanta City Council. Yet, a segment of leadership continued on a conventional and predictable path in which the state seeking militarized policing prevailed through the "democratic process." Reportedly at least $100k was spent to gather over 100,000 signatures for a petition calling upon the Atlanta City council to stop the bulldozing of forests in a Black neighborhood to build Cop City. If those resources had gone into a massive national digital public education campaign, or attorneys for forest protectors, or hiring private security or providing food and support for the communities near the forests … could more creative, subversive and effective interventions manifest?

Activists invested in canceling Cop City are also strongly aligned with demilitarization and decolonization in the U.S., Palestine, and less frequently discussed and addressed, genocidal violence and dispossession of the peoples in Sudan, Congo, and Haiti. In 2024, student peaceful protests on campuses were met with brutal police repression on campuses across the nation. Hyper-militarization expands through U.S. foreign and domestic policies that decimate civil and human rights and foment genocidal wars and occupations, as well as the theft of indigenous peoples' lands, mineral rights, labor, and cultures.

There are unanswered questions about funding in our "movements." "Cop City resistance" remains tied to nonprofits to some degree. Hundreds of millions of (non) corporate dollars followed the 2020 protests in the wake of George Floyd's killing by a police officer in Minneapolis, MN. Despite the protests, U.S. police killings of civilians have increased, and police budgets have expanded.[5]

Funding against predatory policing and imprisonment also continues; yet the productivity of that funding is being questioned. In March 2024, investigative reporters at *Rolling Stone* and *Mother Jones* raised queries or skepticisms about funding to resist Cop Cities. (*Mother Jones* also published Isabela Dias's April 30, 2024, "How a Few Secret Donors Are Fueling the New Right-Wing Infrastructure.") Analyzing, readers distinguish between facts and caricatures to scrutinize the efficacy of resistance that does not rely on performative or nonprofit-funded politics.[6] Platforms emerging in the wake of protests against predatory policing have, in the last ten years, been funded by nonprofits that center electoral politics and at times privilege elite academics who are not the base of movements grounded in material struggles. Voting the "lesser of two evils" has neither deterred genocide or militarized policing or expansion of varied forms of imprisonment.

It should be noted that the current Biden administration has—as have all U.S. administrations—funded the apartheid occupation of Palestine (previous U.S. administrations funded mercenaries to maintain apartheid in South Africa). At the date of writing this introduction, we can note that the U.S. has funded the violent deaths of 34,000 Palestinians after Hamas's October 2023 raid that killed over 1,200 Israelis and foreigners. All life is precious. All predatory regimes must end.

Cop Cities, shaped by premature and violent death, as well as dispossession and dishonor, continue to expand under liber-democratic and reactional-republican administrations. Both U.S. majority parties promote presidential candidates amenable or committed to conquest, colonial warfare, domestic repression, and militarized police and prisons. This text shares political theory, interviews, art, critiques of religion, class warfare, and racism in order to map the evils we seek to confront and quell. This book, *Beyond Cop Cities*, seeks to support principled organizers, activists, and those arrested or facing trials; it resists the continued persecution of political prisoners who fought in freedom struggles only to have the state attempt to disappear them behind concrete prison walls.*

Environmental protectors imprisoned and terrorized with "domestic terrorism" charges must also be fully supported. Those abused by the state must be released into supportive communities. We study, connect, and protect international struggles and liberations for a balanced world. We oppose war, starvation, exploitation, militarized tech investments, and the abuse of nonbinary/trans, children, women, men, and support spiritual/multi-faith practitioners who shelter sacred natural environments, ecosystems, and human life. Captive Maternal[7] stages of struggle suggest that care, protest, movements, marronage, war resistance, and sanctuary are part of the freedom trail that allows us to plant pathways and trajectories to free ourselves and create zones of shared peace, with collective power.

—Joy James

---

* See www.thejerichomovement.com/prisoners to learn more about and support: Mumia Abu-Jamal, Leonard Peltier, Jamil Abdullah Al-Amin, Kamau Sadiki, Rev. Joy Power, Veronza Bowers, Bill Dunne, and other political prisoners. Also in need of support are international prisoners and prisoners of war.

PART I

May 2023 drone photo of destruction of Weelaunee Forest in
Dekalb County, Georgia, USA.
(Source: Instagram. www.instagram.com/stopcopcity/reel/CwYUyOZIl93/)

The Rubik's Cube of Cop City: The Crisis of Colonized Cities and State Criminality

Joy James and Kalonji Jama Changa[1]

I am cognizant of the interrelatedness of all communities and states. I cannot sit idly by in Atlanta. Injustice anywhere is a threat to justice everywhere. We are caught in an inescapable network of mutuality, tied in a single garment of destiny. Whatever affects one directly, affects all indirectly. Never again can we afford to live with the narrow, provincial "outside agitator" idea… You deplore the demonstrations that are presently taking place but your statement, I am sorry to say, fails to express a similar concern for the conditions that brought about the demonstrations.

— Rev. Martin Luther King, Jr., "Letter from a Birmingham Jail," April 16, 1963

When foundations and corporations attempt to run the world by buying politicians and police forces, what's the role of ethical citizenry and captives? How do citizens and captives comprehend the scope and strategies to resist the massive engineering of predatory policing – a rising urban phenomenon that reveals that the term "military occupation" is more than a metaphor, and reaches way beyond any particular city? And when such violence is deployed against citizens by the police, who are protected by the government, who then protects the citizen and captive from this state criminality, which is approved and funded by corporations and the wealthy?

These are questions we invite readers to consider in a set of paired essays about ongoing attempts in Atlanta, Georgia, USA to fund and build a massive new police training center where law enforcement will practice counterinsurgency techniques to use against the city's own citizens. In this first part, we review the militaristic and legal violence that police have been unleashing against people who dare to oppose the new facility, and examine how the Atlanta Police Foundation (APF) draws on vast private wealth to set public policy against the public's wishes. In a second essay, "Urban Warfare and Corporate-Funded Armies," we examine how these strategies practice a form of domestic colonialism with techniques rooted in imperial counterinsurgency.

The Atlanta Police Foundation (APF) is a private foundation with strong corporate ties that supports the Atlanta Police Department. As a private nonprofit, it steers Atlanta policing policy with zero public accountability. APF's promotional tag – "21st Century Community Policing" – suggests concern for non-elite communities. But the language APF uses to describe the aim of the Atlanta Public Safety Training Center – commonly known as "Cop City" – actually presents a lethal Trojan Horse as a humanitarian gift "to make Atlanta the safest large city in the nation." Without specifying the beneficiaries, APF boasts that it will bring "resources to underserved neighborhoods" that are already underfunded and overpoliced – or overpoliced because they are underfunded. APF also claims that it will "cultivate a mindset of true servanthood" within the Atlanta Police Department (APD). What does APF's twisted vision of "true servanthood" look like in practice?

In January 2023 Atlanta state troopers shot and killed Manuel "Tortuguita" Esteban Paez Terán, a 26-year-old environmental activist who was protesting the destruction of ancestral forests to build Cop City. Police claimed that Tortuguita had fired a gun at them, but a private autopsy informed the public that Tortuguita had been sitting cross-legged on the ground with their hands raised when Georgia troopers shot them 57 times.[2] While riddling Tortuguita's body with bullets, a Georgia state trooper was shot and injured, almost certainly by "friendly fire" from another officer.[3] After the killing, organizers obtained public information about the police involved in the shooting and distributed flyers in the neighborhood where one of the officer's lived. Police jailed them on stalking and felony intimidation for sharing this public information with the community.[4]

Organizing food support for families and communities in Atlanta for months, Tortuguita and their collectives provided what the city withheld. Their murder and the subsequent arrests are part of an organized campaign to terrify and jail all who oppose the building of Cop City. In March 2023, prosecutors also charged twenty-three people with domestic terrorism after clashes between police and protesters at the proposed site of Cop City.[5] At the end of May 2023, a police SWAT team, in full gear and weapons, raided the Atlanta Solidarity Fund (a community bail fund), arresting three of its leaders, Marlon Scott Kautz, Adele MacLean, and Savannah D. Patterson.[6] The three have been charged with money laundering and charity fraud, accused of "misleading contributors" to channel funds to the Defend the Atlanta Forest, which was, according to the warrant, "classified by the United States Department of Homeland Security as Domestic Violent Extremists."[7] In fact, the Department of Homeland Security never designated Defend the Atlanta Forest or other community caretakers as "Domestic Violent Extremists." Yet that did not stop DeKalb County Superior Court Judge Shondeana Morris, a Black woman appointed by Republican governor Brian Kemp, from signing the warrant.[8] The warrants claim that the "illegal" reimbursements included expenses for "forest clean-up, totes, covid rapid tests, media, yard signs." The Atlanta Solidarity Fund issued a statement saying that its sole function is to provide resources to protesters facing repression. Following the arrests, the National Lawyers Guild (NLG) released a statement asserting that bail funds protect the right to dissent and to have access to counsel. On June 2, Judge James Altman granted bail.[9]

In June 2020 an Atlanta police officer shot and killed Rayshard Brooks, less than a month after George Floyd was killed in Minneapolis, Minnesota. Brooks's funeral was held at Reverend Martin Luther King, Jr.'s Ebenezer Baptist Church. King's daughter Bernice King and Reverend Raphael Warnock, then a U.S. Senate candidate, addressed the funeral gathering and the public. Warnock spoke eloquently in the historic church: "Rayshard Brooks is the latest high-profile casualty in the struggle for justice and a battle for the soul of America. This is about him but it is so much bigger than him." Neither of Georgia's democratic senators – Warnock and Jon Ossoff – spoke of a "battle for the soul of America" when three years later Georgia troopers assassinated Tortuguita in the forest.

When the twenty-three environmental activists were arrested, Senator Ossoff deplored the "violence" of an "extremist minority"; he did not address the lethal anti-human violence of the Georgia state troopers under the control of Governor Kemp, who rages about terrorism without acknowledging to the public the functions of his Georgia troops.[10] Both senators expressed concerns about the arrests of the organizers of the Atlanta Solidarity Fund; yet they never articulated or advocated for a constitutional right not to be assassinated by police forces.[11] If no one is policing the police for the safety of the community, then security as community care becomes high priority. As public referenda (or even recalls) are waged, electoral politics and legalism appear insufficient in demilitarizing a war zone built and protected by the state with the backing of corporations.

At the June 5–6, 2023, Atlanta City Hall hearing, hundreds of residents – varying in age, race, gender, and income – denounced Cop City for fifteen hours.[12] Despite considerable opposition from the public and community organizers, on June 6, in an 11–4 decision, the Atlanta City Council approved $67 million in funding for the Cop City project. The total cost is anticipated to be $90 million.[13] On June 7, opponents of Cop City filed a petition to create a ballot measure that would ask voters to halt the building of the complex.[14] On June 20, they filed a lawsuit against acting city clerk Vanessa Waldron for delaying certification of the petition. Shortly thereafter, Waldron certified the petition.[15] The petition must now receive signatures from 70,000 Atlanta voters – some argue that the number is closer to 100,000, given likely challenges – by August 15 to be certified and added to the ballot. The referendum petition seeks to repeal the ordinance which authorized the city to lease the eighty-five-acre Intrenchment Creek Park – renamed Weelaunee People's Park by organizers – for the building of Cop City.[16] Cop City is slated to be built on part of what the Muscogee Creek called the Weelaunee forest before state-sponsored terrorism forced them from the lands in the 1820s and 1830s.[17] Before it was a park, now reclaimed by organizers as a forest for food and gardens, it was used by the state of Georgia as a prison farm, on which convict laborers were enslaved growing food for other inmates. Before that it was a plantation. Through duplicitous and antidemocratic politics, federal, state, and local politicians – along with the APF, ADP, and corporate sponsors – plan to dismember the Weelaunee forest into a training ground for war.

APF promises the enhancement of civilian safety through private funding. Yet, the "public–private partnership model" that APF celebrates is more accurately described as a raid on public coffers that will deprive working-class Black Atlantans while building equity for white billionaires and corporations. Atlanta's city council has pledged millions of dollars to bankroll the endeavor. Black citizens are being priced out of a city that they can no longer afford to live within in part because public monies are going to fund a military playground where police will be taught counterinsurgency tactics that could be used to kill Black Atlantans.

Pushed by the APF, under the guise of a public project, Cop City is heavily backed by corporate interests. APF has notable financial and leadership ties to a long list of companies, including Waffle House, Equifax, UPS, Wells Fargo, Home Depot, AT&T, Delta Airlines, Chick-fil-A, and Koch Industries. Cox Enterprises, Inc., a multi-billion-dollar privately held communications corporation that shapes public perceptions, is recognized as a lead funder of Cop City. (In a July 2023 Black Power Media/ Renegade Siafu TV [BPM/RSTV] interview, a member of the Cox family and a member of Atlanta Black clergy critique their respective institutions.) Atlanta's elected officials – its mayor, chief of police, and city councilors – are attentive to the directives of the APF, the brain trust building, banking, and redefining Atlanta through Cop City. APF's website boasts that President Obama's 2015 Task Force on 21st Century Policing promoted Atlanta as a "model city," claiming that it is one of only fifteen juris-dictions out of 18,000 police forces that received such an honor. Celebrating this endorsement from the first Black president veils the fact that the Atlanta democratic politi-cal figures rooting for Cop City are Black but the funders are white corporations. According to the APF, the police training received at Cop City will "improve morale... for APD."[18] How so? Training in domination, violence, and abuse of power increases civilian distrust of policing.

Despite the massive protests in the wake of George Floyd's 2020 death at the hands (or knee) of a Minne-apolis police officer, police killings reached an all-time high in 2022.[19] Simultaneously, APD lost police after the 2020 protests; it plans to hire 750 officers over three years with retention bonuses and relocation stipends.[20] Mayor Andre Dickens maligned environmental and community protectors protesting Cop City by calling them "outsiders" – but APD's growth requires recruiting "outsider" police to accelerate gentrification.

APF sells its product: policing. Meanwhile Atlanta citizens go without bus shelters, well-funded schools, free lunches for children and elders, adequate housing and health care, clean air, and parks. APF sees the forest (and the city budget) as the property not of the public but of affluent sectors and corporate wealth, whose interests are served by the comprador class. People sleep in substandard public housing, or on cardboard in streets and alleys, with insufficient food and care, while investors build a political economy based on predatory policing. Once built, Cop City would train APD, state, regional, and international law enforcement agencies "in 21st Century Policing best practices" while also providing a cushy "gathering spot for community events and conversations" amid the destruction of Black communities through terrorizing those communities and the environmentalists and caretakers protecting them.[21]

Despite its stated mission to care for (Black) youth, the APF still projects them as primary targets of the combined forces of the APD, Fulton County District Attorney, judges, and Atlanta Criminal Justice Commission which will "address Atlanta's repeat offender issue." APF promises "Youth Engagement" to "expand its At-Promise youth initiative" to "divert Atlanta youth from crime to brighter pathways."[22] When nonprofits partner with police (or carceral foster care) to help youth in communities neglected by the city government and abused by predatory policing, they actually worsen the health outcomes of these communities. Artist Hausson Byrd's spoken-word meditation "Projection" poetically addresses the violence of predatory policing. Police networks, as Byrd notes, project their violence upon civilians, citizens, and captives. The disproportionately targeted are poor, working class, and people of color. Rather than ask communities what forms of assistance are useful, governance dictates to under-resourced communities, and continues to destabilize them through financial neglect and punitive policing.

If militarized policing is a colonizing project for cities writ large, it is imperative to think beyond the plans and protests of individual cities, and political betrayals, in order to map trajectories that inform war resistance strategies.

CHAPTER TWO

Urban Warfare and Corporate-Funded Armies: Cop City as a Chapter in the Long History of U.S. Colonialism

Joy James and Kalonji Jama Changa

In the preceding pages, we explored how the Atlanta Police Foundation (APF) – a private, militarized policy offshoot of the Atlanta Police Department (APD) working in collaboration with corporate interests, clergy, and Atlanta City Hall – is forcing the Cop City complex onto Atlanta despite widespread opposition.[1]

What is happening in Georgia right now, however, is not restricted to Atlanta and APF. No one fully has a clear sight of the puppet masters' hands and the manipulation of governance. Still, federal police have a significant impact throughout the country. In July 2022, the FBI raided the St. Louis and St. Petersburg headquarters of Uhuru House, part of the African People's Socialist Party, with weapons drawn, and confiscated files. The raids were conducted supposedly to investigate Russian election interference. But the African People's Socialist Party, which provides food and material support for under-resourced organizations, has noted how the FBI's use of the Foreign Agents Registration Act (FARA) is continuous with its long history of violent policing against environmentalists at the behest of corporations.[2] The FBI appears to maintain a similar appetite to that wielded by J. Edgar Hoover under the COINTELPRO program which, with lethal efficiency, sabotaged Black radical organizing.[3]

What we are witnessing is the logic of colonialism practiced domestically. Colonialism is a contemporary threat to the stability of cities (and countries) facing attempts by corporations and governments to violate the rights of working-class and low-income communities, most often Black and brown. Addressing the complexity or puzzle of Cop City means acknowledging the historical trajectory of militarized violence, corporate dominance, and political corruption that preceded the present crisis.

Paramilitary and mercenary foreign policy strategies seep into domestic policing. Six decades ago, Democratic and Republican administrations were both equally funding white mercenaries and paramilitary policing to destabilize African freedom movements. In 1964, President Lyndon Johnson authorized the Department of Defense to provide material support toward the effort of undermining and killing African liberation leaders and intellectuals.[4] This racial terrorism in U.S. foreign policy was coterminous with domestic policy. Despite the terror, Black agency continued to resist violence and dishonor.[5]

In the summer of 1964, Johnson met with the parents of slain white civil rights activists Andrew Goodman and Michael Schwerner, but seemingly not with the parents of James Chaney, a Black Mississippi CORE organizer.[6] That June, assisted by a sheriff's deputy, Klansmen had assassinated the three civil rights workers in Mississippi and buried the bodies in a dam. Johnson called upon J. Edgar Hoover to solve the crime. The corpses were found on August 4, 1964, when President Johnson was campaigning for the presidency and attempting to appease various political factions. During the search for the bodies of the civil rights activists, rivers were dragged and eight corpses of Black males discovered, including two nineteen-year-olds and one fourteen-year-old who was wearing a Congress of Racial Equality (CORE) T-shirt.[7] On August 3, 1980, one day short of the sixteenth anniversary of the recovery of the bodies of the murdered civil rights activists, Republican presidential candidate Ronald Reagan, staging his campaign near Philadelphia, Mississippi, a ten-minute drive from the dam where the three organizers had been buried, stood at the podium demanding "state's rights."

History is instructive. Atlanta's brutalities and tragedies are not unique. Cop City's current paramilitary violence – from city police, state troopers, and the FBI – mirrors the lethal policies of the past where vigilante and police terror, opportunist politicians, and state criminality converged. Without the formal endorsement of (white) nationalist presidential candidates such as Donald Trump and Ron DeSantis, Black compradors have worked in and beyond Atlanta to obscure the legacies of Martin Luther King, Jr., el-Hajj Malik el-Shabazz (Malcolm X), Fannie Lou Hamer, Rosa Parks, and Ella Baker. Investment portfolios incentivized by corporations and foundations seek to decimate the civil rights of working-class and poor communities deemed exploitable and expendable, particularly if they are Black. From city councils to mayors, through governors, Congress, and the White House, intimidation and terror tactics appear to be implicitly (by Democrats) and explicitly (by Republicans) approved in standard governance for the control of Black cities and communities.

APF is only one organization within a larger nexus of "public–private" partnerships attempting to shape Atlanta's public safety policies. Headquartered inside the Andrew

Young School of Policy Studies at Georgia State University, the Georgia International Law Enforcement Exchange (GILEE) has been in partnership with the university, Atlanta Police Department (as well as various other police agencies), public and corporate sectors, and civic groups since its inception thirty years ago. Among its activities, GILEE organizes a police exchange program that provides U.S. law enforcement with special training from Israeli police.[8] Aside from hosting Atlanta police, the *Jerusalem Post* reports that "Israel… has hosted over 1,200 public safety officials since the start of the program."[9] A least twenty-nine U.S. delegations of law enforcement have traveled to Jerusalem to participate in "intensive two-week training programs," including many from the Atlanta area.

Why would Atlanta, a city that many view as the "civil rights capital," look to Israel for local police training – and what does this training even consist of?[10]

In 2019 the United Nations Human Rights Council released a twenty-two-page report stating, according to the *New York Times*, that "Israeli troops may have committed crimes against humanity in shooting unarmed civilians – including children – who posed no threat during mass protests."[11] Israeli military and police forces have been guilty of the illegal occupation of Palestine for the last fifty-six years – making it, according to law scholar Valentina Azarova, the longest occupation in modern history.[12] They have a well-documented track record of human rights abuses. Yet for the past three decades the Atlanta Police Department, as well as various state and local officials, have through GILEE turned to these same actors to train law enforcement in military tactics in Georgia.

GILEE donations, channeled through Georgia State University and government funding, are more opaque than

APF resources. We know, though, that APF is supported by major corporations such as Cox Media Group, Coca Cola, Wells Fargo, Delta, and Home Depot.[13] A host of other multinational corporations maintain a significant influence in and beyond Atlanta by funneling private funding into police foundations. Deploying similar tactics across the globe, U.S. corporations have facilitated coups and assassinations of labor, environmental, and human rights organizers in Haiti, Guatemala, Nicaragua, and many other nations.[14] In its refusal to hear an impassioned citizenry argue and plead against a militarized zone, Atlanta remains loyal to the trajectory of colonial cities despite the rising costs and violence against civilians.

A member of Atlanta's Faith Coalition to Stop Cop City, Reverend Keyanna Jones has family that lives in the Black neighborhood targeted for gentrification and militarization through Cop City.[15] In her activism against the police training complex, Rev. Jones brings attention to the betrayals of Black mayors and the predominately Black city council. Jones and other activists have drawn attention to the fact that plans for Cop City include a "mock village" in which police will practice urban warfare tactics.[16] Contributors to educational platforms such as *Scalawag* help keep the public informed on strategic opposition to state warfare.

Rev. Jones anticipates that Cop City will be used for police training in "MOUT" tactics. MOUT is a genre of military-developed urban warfare strategies – for example, as described in the Marines-developed training handbook, *Military Operations on Urban Terrain (MOUT).*[17] The manual focuses on "military operations on urbanized terrain" (i.e. urban warfare), with diagrams illustrating military operations in commercial and residential areas that would be perfectly at home in Atlanta. Indeed, an Army report from the early 1980s says that researchers developing MOUT techniques used the city of Atlanta as a basis for their research.[18] Under the rubric of MOUT, protests against police violence, redistricting, poverty, and hunger become criminalized. Essentially, communal advocacy and protests for civil and human rights are treated as acts of terrorism. This is the Atlanta (and international) playbook to colonize a city. In its effort to suppress dissent against Cop City, the majority of Atlanta's city government has criminalized people who want to grow flowers and food, and attend music festivals and, while there, show solidarity with forest protectors without being arrested on "terrorist" charges.

The U.S. military has practiced some version of MOUT across the globe for decades. Combat training seeks to colonize your local city. Primary targets of the domestic deployment of MOUT will be Black folks, BIPOC, and working-class and low-income communities. Some argue that the "asymmetric enemy" will look like the "Chocolate City" or "Black Mecca" and thus we should expect some version of Detroit 1967 in the future. State violence continues despite the fact that it would be simpler, safer, and more orderly to provide healthy jobs, food, housing, schooling, and green spaces to communities. Progressives' and abolitionists' unpreparedness for repressive mandates to construct and control "internal colonies" indicates that this ongoing struggle has been shortsightedly portrayed as a local, urban issue.

Speaking about Atlanta during a June 9, 2023, *Black Power Media* (*BPM*) podcast, this essay's coauthor, Kalonji Changa, reflected upon the trajectory of escalating state violence and police as executioners:

23

The arrogant and desperate attempt to terrorize and crush the morale of activists five days before the Atlanta City Council's vote on funding the corporate-sponsored paramilitary training ground is utterly repulsive. The trumped-up charges used to criminalize and vilify the Atlanta Solidarity Fund's legitimate activists, including Marlon Kautz, and Adele MacLean – both of whom I have known and organized with for well over a decade – is proof that these warmongers will pull out all stops to achieve their goals. The police and the media have unsuccessfully tried to paint Marlon and Adele as opportunists or "agitators" when in fact they are seasoned organizers who have a long history of organizing in the Atlanta community. As part of their Cop Watch program, they worked alongside our organization, The FTP Movement, and many other organizations working on numerous campaigns, including the case of Troy Anthony Davis who was executed in September 2011 despite global demands for a stay due to his innocence. The state's blatant disregard for community will be their ultimate demise. You *cannot* attack community organizers in front of the world and think that it will be an easy victory.

Cop City's architects have blood on their hands for the murder of Tortuguita. The government and police should be charged not only with his assassination, but also the numerous false arrests, bullying, scare tactics, and the strong-armed robbery of taxpayers who are supposed to provide the tens of millions to fund a colonial project. The APF, corporate donors, and indifferent Georgia politicians are the true domestic terrorists.

Activists warn that a militarized police training center will disenfranchise a Black working-class community as the state and corporations wage a lethal war against communities and civilians. The only people killed or tortured in Atlanta were those assaulted by police. Communities deploy various strategies in war resistance. Anti-colonial battles are continuous and require constant vigilance. Less than a two-hour drive from Atlanta, at Fort Benning, another deadly entity with a benign name – the School of the Americas (SOA), also known as the "School of the Assassins" – was shut down by ethical organizers in 2000.[19] Yet the former SOA was rebranded as the Western Hemisphere Institute for Security Cooperation, which reportedly continues to offer SOA's curriculum of torture, assassinations, and human rights violations. Still, mass gatherings of diverse and principled individuals and communities continue to resist death and gentrification structured by communal dispossession, predatory policing, and state criminality from New York to Nanterre. History remains instructive.[20] In 1972, only a few months before his assassination in Guinea by forces supporting colonialism, African liberator Amílcar Cabral spoke with New York City organizers (his speech is preserved in *Return to the Source*), instructing and offering international solidarity in anti-colonial war resistance:

We realize the difficulties you face, the problems you have and your feelings, your revolts, and also your hopes. We think that our fighting for Africa against colonialism and imperialism is a proof of understanding of your problem and also a contribution for the solution of your problems in this continent. Naturally, the inverse is also true.[21]

25

CHAPTER THREE

A Letter of Concern to Black Clergy Regarding "Cop City"[1]

Reverend Matthew V. Johnson and Joy James

Introduction: Joy James

Last March [2023], I spoke at a University of Michigan conference, titled "Insurgent Research: Practice and Theory," organized by Comp Lit doctoral students. The conference flyer showed a photograph of Atlanta protests against "Cop City" and a banner with the image of Tortuguita (Manuel Paez Terán), who was assassinated by Georgia state troopers in January 2023, while they sat unarmed with their hands in the air. After police forces slandered Tortuguita, falsely stating that they had shot a trooper in the leg, the traumatized family released the private autopsy: Troopers shot the meditating forest protector/communal caretaker 57 times. (People registered their concerns with Georgia State Patrol, https://dps. georgia.gov/divisions/georgia-state-patrol.)

My talk in Ann Arbor focused on resistance to (proto) fascism, from Mao's 1941 statement on the "united front against fascism" through the Black Panther Party and Students for a Democratic Society 1969 attempts to fashion a united front against U.S. fascism and the Federal Bureau of Investigation (FBI) to the Black communities' rights to self-defense today. As local police forces increased their use of lethal force and assassinations to derail freedom movements, a student conference table offered diverse literature and postcards for those swept up in mass arrests during and after the Atlanta music festival where police and the Georgia Bureau of Investigation (GBI) levied unsubstantiated "terrorism" charges against activists and advocates enjoying cultural events.

Several weeks after the conference, I travelled to Atlanta for an *In Pursuit of Revolutionary Love* book talk with beloved comrades working with ARC on reproductive rights and protections for LGBTQIA+ communities. In Atlanta, I met with forest protectors who knew Michigan students. At a café, over tea, Reverend Matthew (whose brilliant missive appears below), a young Black (fe)male anarchist, and I reflected on how best to cope with and minimize tragedies inflicted by state violence.

During the conversation, I asked about security strategies for forest/community protectors and war resisters. I wondered aloud how to magnify concentric circles to protect the epicenter where risk-taking and Agape-driven actors hold space to shield Black working-class communities adjacent to the forest and gardens from a former prison farm and plantation (one would think that reparations due would allow the community to keep its communal lands).

Activists are routinely brutalized or disappeared by predatory city/county/state/federal police forces. While those devoted organizers hold the core, how might we as local, national, international communities and organizers increase our capacity to build rings of concentric circles that mobilize medical, legal, media, and security to deflect state violence. Working to cushion the blows of predatory policing, how can I and my kin in outer rings deliver encompassing care and forms of security that radiate from the local community through the city, state, nation, and international communities in ways that aid war resisters and deter predatory police forces. The proverbial ripples from the pebble thrown into the pond make legible movements that radiate beyond the spot in which the pebble drops.

Dishonor and torture by state violence will continue; so, we must provide security rings to deflect blows. We best face the predatory state by committing to encircle each other in care. Those who take the most risks to resist war should receive the most resources for self-defense. Conventional politicians – mayors and city councils – dishonor and endanger our lives, lands, and loved ones. Their mammon-like appetites for prestige and power – from payouts to pulpits and presidential politics – must be contained. Our devotion to the Beloved Community, despite our fears, will align with Agape – love as political will. We have capacity for struggles in diverse zones that interconnect caretaking, protests, movements, marronage, and war resistance.

Reverend Martin Luther King, Jr. wrote in his August 1963 "Letter from Birmingham Jail": "I am cognizant of the interrelatedness of all communities and states. I cannot sit idly by in Atlanta… Injustice anywhere is a threat to justice everywhere." Just as King saw it sixty years ago, this is an *international* struggle. The militarization of forests and gentrification of Black working-class communities reflect corporate and colonial ambitions. Police violence, arrests, and executions disproportionately target Black/brown poor and working-classes. The militarization of society strips public funding for decent housing, education, food, employment, and culture and redirects funds towards entities such as the police foundations, and corporate entities.

Black/brown compradors will continue to cash in on the colonization of cities until they are forced to stop their exploitation and greed. A security apparatus can protect not only lives but also international boycotts, recalls, referendums, primarying incumbents bought by corporations and military industries. Increasingly forced into marronage, with the theft of lands, waters and collective reparations, we mutate to better figure out how political kin and communities build concentric care and security. Officialdom marches the mass and communal caretakers into muddy waters. Through agency as Captive Maternals, we retain capacity to wade and evade the cesspools created by corporate donors and compradors.

Reverend Matthew V. Johnson

Dear Siblings in the Faith,

I am writing to you during this Lenten season from my home in Atlanta. I write with a heavy heart, having lost friends to jail under false charges and one to murder, covered up poorly by police. I pray without ceasing for those who are still under arrest, denied bail, deemed a threat to the community for no good reason. I pray that the mother of the slain, Belkis Terán, a devout Catholic, know who her child truly was, despite the misinformation swirling around their death. Tortuguita was murdered, shot over a dozen times with their hands raised and their legs crossed. May the bullet holes through their palms, holy stigmata, be a reminder that their child was a servant of God.

In Atlanta, we find ourselves in a struggle at the intersection of climate change, police militarization, racialized police violence, and environmental racism: The movement to Defend the Atlanta Forest and to Stop Cop City. I have never been so certain that Jesus is guiding my path, but that path has most often been far from the church. That is certainly not Jesus's problem, nor do I believe that it is a me-problem, but after much reflection and patience, I have come to believe that it is Atlanta's well-established Black churches that ought to examine themselves. After two years of protest, a year and a half of a forest occupation, over forty people arrested for domestic terrorism without one injury to a living being, and a murder by police, the only thing that stirred respectable Black Clergy to mumble a word was the destruction of property being used to flout the will of the people most affected. Many others remain silent.

Now is not a time for silence. In order to curry favor and privilege with corporate interests and Black faces in high places, Atlanta's Black churches have been silent for decades of iniquity. Whatever they have gained is miniscule in comparison to the amount of wealth, opportunity, and life chances expropriated from the Black masses who continue to build this city. The time for silence in the face of systemic injustice in exchange for a few sterling examples of Black Excellence is over. I do not come to this conclusion lightly, and I have been back home in Atlanta since 2019 before I chose to say one word of criticism. Before I return to speak to the moment, I would like to give more context for my position.

Atlanta's racial consciousness exists with a profound cognitive dissonance. On one hand, we are proud to elect politicians, appoint government officials, and promote some corporate leaders from Atlanta's Black population. On the other hand, we are not blind to the fact that these immense efforts failed to stem the tide of inequality and systemic injustice that maintain the largest racial income gap of a major city in the United States. While we do not want to call out our folk who "made it," we begin to wonder whether these *leaders* are unable or unwilling to make the changes we need. While we hoped they would bring us closer to liberation, it too often appears that these Black *leaders*' position, power, and status is predicated on their ability and willingness to keep the rest of us in line. Greater disparities in wealth and increasing state violence show cracks in this façade of peace and raise questions about the veracity of this oft-repeated claim of Atlanta as the Black Mecca. The city's inability to curb unrest and national, state, and local unwillingness to allocate resources to social programs creates the tenor where the wealthy and corporations see the development of a militarized police training facility as the only means to keep themselves safe. The false scarcity and unresponsiveness to the needs of the people created by corporate greed necessitates the state violence required to maintain itself. This is the role that the police are being trained to fulfill. Continued investment in this cycle of violence will only perpetuate violence and the widening gap between haves and have-nots.

In order to push forward these widely unpopular ideas, the wealthy and powerful send the Black Political Class and a host of pre-approved community *leaders* who are ingratiated to them.

Whether it is for wealth, power, status, or for continued patronage of valuable community work, Black *leaders* often make political compromises deleterious to the Black masses in order to, at best, benefit a small segment of our people. After watching the Concerned Black Clergy of Metropolitan Atlanta mobilize so quickly in 2023 on March 10, following interfaith leaders gathering on March 6 in front of City Hall, and a Black activist-led mobilization on March 9, it was dreadfully obvious what their role was. They came to stamp out opposition to a militarized police training facility in a Black neighborhood already feeling disproportionate impact of environmental degradation. Let's be clear: no matter how many Black clergy or politicians they put in front of this project, the wealthy private citizens, ownership of the corporations, and decision-makers of foundations that support this project are *overwhelmingly White*. They simply have the resources to buy off more influential Black people to put out front to mislead others. We cannot allow our elders to invoke the Civil Rights struggles of the 1960s to disparage the struggles and tactics of a completely different time without scrutiny in the name of respectability. It is time we ask our heroes of yesteryear what they are doing now if they continue to act as representatives of our people in the present.

We often find a subtle contradiction among such senior clergy: If you have been so deeply involved and connected to the system, how on Earth did things get so bad? Why on Earth should we believe that you are the people that will be able to do a new thing? I question the fitness of past generations to speak to the popular struggles of the past decade.

2 Timothy 2:15: I do not come to ministry lightly. By virtue of the assignment, being ordained implies that you accepted a calling to speak on behalf of the most powerful being in the universe, the most expansive being and thought that any being could ever conceive of. In order

to take such an assignment, you must be certain, arrogant beyond belief, out of your mind, or not believe that God exists. I am certain of that call, and I know that God exists (I am open to arguments that I am arrogant or out of mind). Nevertheless, I fully understand the assignment, and I have worked for some time to prepare myself for it as best as I could.

I am no outside agitator. I attended Morehouse College where I was president of the debate team and a coach of Grady High School's speech and debate team years before God called me. My basis for understanding the world around me was firmly grounded in reason. When God spoke to me, I examined every other possibility of my experience. When I knew it was God, I spent years learning about the world around me and learning skills outside of church walls before I was led to pursue graduate education to prepare for ministry. I received a Master of Divinity from the University of Chicago and returned to Atlanta in the summer of 2019.

By January 2019, I woke up in Hyde Park performing my morning prayers facing south. I knew God was calling me back to Atlanta many months before I returned. I faced significant harassment when I was in Chicago. This was not simply for holding my political and theological beliefs; my real offence was my commitment to learning the requisite skills and competencies to actualize the societal changes I spoke about. I have been all too familiar with ministers who spoke to the concerns of Black people but lacked interest, capacity, will, skill, or knowledge to enact the changes they talked about. These people are not a threat to the system; they say all the right things but cannot execute any of them. I resolved within myself to prepare as best I could to build a world in line with

33

the vision of societal transformation Jesus cast. I do not believe such work to educate oneself ever stops, and I have continued to learn, prepare, and practice in ways that are reflective of the world I want to see. Certainly, missing the mark far more than I could ever embody the Gospel of Jesus Christ, I have tried my best to understand who Jesus was and find out how to follow his example. I am afraid that too many of our co-laborers spent more time building a platform to reach people without the foundation to know what to tell them once they had their ears.

When I returned to Atlanta in the summer of 2019, a local pastor of a well-established Black church whom I knew from family connections asked me to preach for him. He explained to me that a member whom he never knew to have means gave $25,000 on the Sunday I visited in the spring. I sat by the man and we spoke that Sunday, and the pastor even said that he saw me as something of a "good luck charm." Although I was not yet convinced that this was where I should stay, I decided that it was where I would plant my feet as I discerned next steps in ministry.

I remember the Sunday after the George Floyd Rebellions started and I attempted to explain what I saw near the CNN Center. I saw police firing pepper spray indiscriminately, using violence disproportionately with no adequate response to people emboldened to protest their treatment *en masse*. Even if the reader believes that arbitrary violence against people is a reasonable response to property destruction, I left that evening before any police cars were set on fire. What I saw was wrong done by police that were panicked, but unlike other people who use violence when they are panicked, law enforcement officers are protected by the state and do not lose years of their lives in prison when they make such mistakes.

In the face of the largest demonstrations against state violence in the recorded history of the Earth, my pastor gave a quippy one-liner and moved on with his sermon as if the world was not burning all around him. Although I had been teaching Wednesday night Bible studies almost every week for the past two months of the pandemic, those weekly invitations disappeared. Perhaps we both knew that my assignment and this well-established church would not align.

Shortly after Rayshard Brooks was murdered by Atlanta police officer Garrett Rolfe, on June 12, 2020, I met a young activist only armed with a megaphone at a protest that was headed toward APD's Third Precinct. I gave him a respirator since the police liberally used tear gas during protests in those days, and told him that he could reach me if he ever needed support. We stayed in touch, and he asked me to come to Rayshard Brooks's funeral along with him. As we sat in Ebenezer Baptist Church and watched speaker after speaker give their respects and proceed through the program, the young activist looked over to me and said, "Do you think they would have ever welcomed Rayshard here if he weren't killed by the police?" He understood the deep class divide that existed in Atlanta's most internationally known church, the spiritual home of Dr. Martin Luther King, Jr. Such events were politically expedient while Rev. Dr. Warnock was running for office as a progressive, but his critiques of police brutality and militarism faded as Senator Warnock settled into office. That young activist named Antonio Lewis who spoke boldly against police brutality and Cop City on the campaign trail said nothing as Councilman Antonio Lewis. Garret Rolfe, the officer who shot Rayshard Brooks in the back, received backpay and was reinstated as an APD officer.

Now, Councilman Lewis spouts conspiracy theories about protestors sabotaging critical infrastructure as he supports Cop City, pads the pockets of police officers, and funds APF projects that further the surveillance of Black communities. While Warnock and Lewis convinced themselves that they would change things from the inside, it looks like they are the ones who changed. The changes I noticed were police killings across America, the murder rate in Atlanta, and the Atlanta Police budget disproportionately rising since 2020. Our communities are no safer, but Senator Warnock and Councilman Lewis gained notoriety. I expect little from politicians, especially without strong checks from community voices that are willing to hold politicians accountable to what they said they would do before they got in office. I expect the most ardent advocacy from those who commit to the ultimate reality beyond this plane of existence, yet the clergy have let us down yet again in the fight against America's modern, militarized policing apparatus.

Many of the people whom I have organized with over the past three years only learned that I am ordained Baptist clergy in the past few months. Over the past three years, I did not offer unsolicited feedback; I did not tell people how things should be done based on how things were once done; I did not rush to podiums or seek out interviews; I did not assume that I knew the answers simply because I was in a position of influence. Over the past three years, I helped and listened where I saw worthwhile work being done; I asked questions where I did not understand the situation; I waited to speak until we were facing unprecedented repression; I voiced internal criticism and encouraged holistic, critical thinking about our predicament when disagreements on tactics and strategy arose.

This order of operations, based on discernment, empathy, and introspection is more in keeping with the Gospel of Jesus Christ than an approach characterized by bolstering the credibility of worldly power, rash judgement of a movement with little to no research on policing or environmental impact, and a lack of scrutiny or calls for tangible policy change to advance systemic justice. The latter approach is the common characterization of clergy many activists held, informed by their personal experiences.

The ministers who gathered on March 10 in reaction to the Faith Coalition of Forest Defenders and the prior night's Black-led protest to Stop Cop City should be embarrassed to only raise their voices about policing in the United States at this juncture. In Atlanta, we have a Black *leadership* class that became so obsessed with maintaining relationships with people in power, they were willing to sacrifice their responsibility to speak truth to those powers in order to maintain the relationships. This is precisely how you end up with the Blackest city in America having the largest racial income disparity in the country, continually contaminated water supply, widespread displacement of legacy residents, and *corporate outside agitators*, bringing employees from elsewhere at far higher salaries with no tangible benefits to the neighborhoods they settle in, driving up the cost of everything. It appears outsiders only become *agitating* to our government when they are questioning the power structures that legitimate racialized capitalism.

Do not expect me to publicly condemn property destruction of equipment being used to destroy public property against the will of the public. Furthermore, the destruction of this publicly owned land builds capacity for law enforcement that fails to respect the sanctity of human life and a commitment to nonviolence. Police routinely destroy and confiscate protestor-owned property and dole out unreciprocated violence as we wage the fight to Stop Cop City. However, many have deluded themselves into believing that this asymmetrical warfare against the public is justice, and this is reinforced in multiple facets of our society.

People fighting for a better tomorrow with no sanctioned power to defend themselves are consistently faced with moral purity tests in the media while people who have a state-sanctioned monopoly on violence are never asked to commit to nonviolent strategies. The people who have no protection under the law are expected to act with unflinching pacifism while militarized police forces, each receiving millions of dollars to learn to not use excessive force, are constantly given the benefit of the doubt when they do. We are accustomed to the asymmetry of asking people who are part of decentralized movements to justify the tactics of people whom they have no control over, while politicians such as Andre Dickens and Antonio Lewis go without questioning on Garret Rolfe being rehired and receiving backpay from APD. Both supported measures to reallocate police funding and condemned the murder of Rayshard Brooks when it was politically expedient. A government, corporate, media, or clerical apparatus that reinforces such asymmetry has no moral authority to condemn the Movement to Defend the Atlanta Forest and Stop Cop City.

When we see Atlanta City Council and consecutive mayors vote in favor of this training facility and/or refuse to speak out, despite widespread opposition, I have no empirical evidence that the electoral process will reflect the will of the people rather than monied private and corporate influence. When we have seen Ryan Millsap continue work on contested public land after a Dekalb County Stop Work Order, David Wilkinson push forward with a land disturbance permit despite an appeal to Dekalb County, and judges deny bond to protestors with no evidence to deem them a threat to the community, I have no empirical evidence that our judicial system will protect the will of the people. When I have personally dealt with police harassment and repression without committing one crime, I have no empirical evidence to tell activists and organizers that widely accepted means of protest or their innovative strategies will shield them from excessive force or repression. In other words, it is not reason, it is not faith, but a failure of nerve, delusion, or preservation of privileged access that leads clergy to mention systemic injustice in general but condemn individual "sins" of protesters in particular. Such rhetorical strategies work to discredit movements that contain multitudes, while people called to be mouthpieces of God use their moral authority to ingratiate themselves to worldly powers, failing to speak truth to them as they were called to do.

Ecclesiastes 4:13: Despite deep concern with the patterns of engagement I have seen with clergy cozying up to power and privilege rather than investigating these facets of society with a critical eye, I have not directly criticized clergy, especially our elders, affording grace and patience in things that I may not see. Granted, there are many things that I may still not understand, but I have seen enough to know that many of our elders speak out of a lack of knowledge and desire to be associated with power and prestige. I will focus here on conversations I had with Rev. Dr. Gerald Durley and the speech I watched Rev. Timothy McDonald give on March 10. Both are well-esteemed members of the community and members of the Concerned Black Clergy of Metropolitan Atlanta, and from their comments, I believe that these elders could benefit from research and self-reflection.

I noted that I would like to have a deeper conversation with the Concerned Black Clergy, because if we cannot have a reasoned dialogue based on the information, who can? Dr. Durley did not respond to this request but instead questioned me on why I opposed the project. I explained to him the environmental impact and the history of the court cases with the Stop Cop City and Stop the Swap coalitions. He asked where I got my information from. Before I could go into detail about the research I have been doing for two years, he cut me off to tell me the claims I made were "erroneous." He then explained how he worked with groups such as the Sierra Club and Green Peace. I then explained to him that both groups publicly supported the movement to Stop Cop City. He then mentioned other respectable individuals that are supporting the project to which I responded, "I am not a respecter of persons, but I do my research." He then explained that he had to go after he initiated a conversation that I only hoped to schedule for the future.

As it turns out, Rev. Dr. Gerald Durley accepted a seat on the new Advisory Committee for Cop City before we had this conversation. Also, I understand why Dr. Durley would be so quick to dismiss the claims of environmental degradation. The same EPA administrator, Daniel Blackman, who was unresponsive to the South River Watershed Alliance's demand that the Clean Water Act be enforced is on the Board of the Concerned Black Clergy of Metropolitan Atlanta. I am not speaking from a holier-than-thou position; these are difficult times and spaces to navigate. I have often made mistakes, assuming the credibility of close associates when they are acting out of self-preservation, but there is a much greater responsibility for Dr. Durley when the future of a city and her Black People are at stake.

Rev. James Orange would always say "Look out for Antifa!," while Rev. McDonald explained his unwillingness to stand up for those arrested under domestic terrorism charges by painting them with a broad, uninformed brush. Antifa means "Antifascist," which I hope the reverend would consider himself to be. He fails to understand or acknowledge that there has been virtually no evidence tying any jailed individual to violent crime or property destruction. However, simple association with the movement is disagreeable enough for Rev. McDonald.

Given his stance on Cop City, Rev. McDonald does not hold local and state law enforcement and government to nearly the same moral standard whereas they have destroyed evidence, property, and have a long-standing history of assaulting and disappearing activists. Apparently, property destruction on publicly owned land where construction moves forward illegally and undemocratically is where Rev. McDonald takes his moral stance. People identifying themselves as Antifa have been most active protecting Civil Rights protests, far-right counter protests, and LGBTQIA events; I find this caution from Rev. Orange a bit out of place, but I was not there.

We should also note that Rev. James Orange, God rest his soul, died in 2008. If this is the most recent example that Rev. McDonald can think to reference clergy concerns during street protests, he should cede the microphone to clergy that are in better touch with organizers and activists from the past fifteen years.

Concerned Black Clergy state that they see the training facility "as an opportunity for the community to make a template of how we can do law enforcement. Imagine, if you will, the city of Atlanta working with the faith community, working with community organizers, with community leaders, sitting down with law enforcement, and talking about how training ought to look!"

I'm confused. What have the Concerned Black Clergy been doing when sitting down with the City of Atlanta thus far? Why should we believe that a training facility whose infrastructure is geared toward militarized training in real-world cityscapes is needed in order to have conversations with community stakeholders? And if there is already a blueprint for the facility made, what leads Rev. McDonald to believe that they have not already determined what the priorities for training are?

All the things that Rev. McDonald mentions are piecemeal reforms that many people with close ties to government officials from the Black Community promised before, and it never amounts to anything. Meanwhile, police budgets have ballooned, the equipment has become more militarized and expensive, while we are no safer. Spending more and more money on policing is not a new thing. Investing in communities and new and creative ways to keep our communities safe is new. That is precisely what we are proposing. Rev. McDonald, on the other hand, is supporting the old system that continues to fail us while promoting reforms people have been promised to no avail.

Concerning "outside agitators" rhetoric, I have heard Black clergy say: "How are you going to have people come in internationally and tell us Atlanta, tax payers, what to do?" This is a statement regarding two people (noncitizens) arrested under domestic terrorism charges.

However, "telling us what to do" is precisely what happens with international corporations in Atlanta endangering our natural resources for their profits. Atlanta was named the most overpriced housing market in the country, prices driven up by investor-owned rental companies, extracting wealth where Black families could be building it. Their aggressive strategies to buy up real estate in Atlanta has increased the burden on the taxpayers in Atlanta, but these issues that do harm to Atlantans are not what Rev. McDonald holds a press conference to address.

These corporate interests have undue influence in our legislation, maintain flat wages for working-class Black families, and pump money into law enforcement foundations that invest in a more punitive, surveillance state rather than social services, receiving tax credits for doing so. International corporations continually work to undercut our social safety net and efforts to secure livable wages while patting themselves on the back for donating a penance of what they have pilfered through policy back into well-meaning nonprofit organizations. In fact, the most common form of theft in the United States is wage theft by employers, but that is not a criminal offense. Police are the frontliners to reinforce these social injustices that rich and powerful private interests reify by expenditure in government and law enforcement.

Matthew 6:21: The question still remains: How did things get this bad with these same ministers being so cozy with power? Engagement in the real world requires nuance and some compromise. However, the world's systems of power and distribution of resources is too far out of balance to think that furthering the capacity for state violence will address our problems. We must seek new ways to address social problems. If it were more gear and more money for police, we would have solved the problem by now. I also understand that many pastors are afraid to speak out because of ties to the criminal justice system and law enforcement that sustain their church. However, if a pastor is qualifying what he/she/they say about injustice to accommodate the powers that be from the pulpit, they already lost the Church of Jesus Christ and their moral authority. Let us honor Atlanta's Prophet, Tortuguita, and the Savior of the World by joining the fight to Stop Cop City.

Dyana Bagby, "'Cop City' protesters and police clash near Atlanta public safety training center site," *Rough Draft Atlanta*, November 13, 2023.

https://roughdraftatlanta.com/2023/11/13/photos-cop-city-protesters-and-police-clash-near-atlanta-public-safety-training-center-site/

CHAPTER FOUR

Resisting Cop City Corporate and Clergy Colonizers

Fergie Chambers, Matt Johnson, Kalonji Changa, and Joy James

Joy James (JJ): For your community, there is no puzzle at all in terms of what Cop City is: militarization, colonialism, death to autonomy and community cultures.

The general population may see it more as a local city and an Atlanta problem, as if it is something isolated and not connected to colonialism. Cop City is global. The U.S. is the most militarized nation in the world; cop cities are engineered and funded by the U.S. Concerning the Rubik's Cube, whether or not you ever played with one as a kid or an adult, you know that you have to put the pieces together to understand that the state's concept of Cop City is not about one city in the South. This is a matrix of global political policies and aspirations for domination; controlling civilian populations; denying human rights (however people want to define or protect them). The militarization of police and the police functioning as paramilitaries means that they globally train; people come from other countries, such as Israel, train in Atlanta. These are the issues that we're tackling in the two-piece article.

Kalonji Changa (KC): Cop City is about new age imperialism... globalization, and this is a small piece, as you mentioned, of that puzzle. I remember as a child when Rubik's Cubes first came out, some of us would take the stickers and we'd try to cheat just to pass our friends. So, we'd take these stickers off, put them elsewhere and claim: "Look, I finished it!" This reminds me of what Atlanta is doing now. They are taking the labels off and shifting things around. To an extent, you find pieces of the puzzle scattered around, but they all fit at the end of the day. We can see where the corporations, educational institutions, local police and police unions are all a part of this large puzzle.

JJ: Every aspect of community and culture can be bought, from your church, through the high school principal, to the academic in the classroom. This is going to be a collective struggle where we will see that our opposition will include people who look very much like us and who, as you say, move the stickers and mask themselves as being concerned about civil rights, working-class people, Black people. It's not true. They are masquerading in care, when really their ambition has to do a lot with money. For the white corporations paying for all this and for the U.S. government, which has quite a bit of white nationalism embedded within it, it is about colonial control.

KC: The first guest, I've seen his work in the Atlanta area and abroad. He's a rather unique comrade. His family would fall into the corporate elite. He is a member of the Berkshire Communist Party. Fergie Chambers, what's happening my man?

Fergie Chambers (FC): Hello, nice to see you. I'm up in the hills of New England, but very much with thoughts on Atlanta.

JJ: Hello, Fergie. What sparked you to become an organizer?

FC: I came from a very wealthy and powerful family. The family firm, and many of the family members are based in Atlanta. I was from New York and Massachusetts, but lived there for some time as well. That is where I got involved directly in organizing, for a few reasons, after having some violent run-ins with the ruling class. One side of my family was not from the upper level of the bourgeoisie... Their revolutionary minds at the time I grew up... gave me some good ideas. I worked for my family's company for one year at an auto auction in Georgia. Then I moved to Atlanta. When Michael Brown was murdered [in 2014 in Ferguson, MO], I more deliberately converted my political ideas into a consistent struggle on the ground. I attended protests as far back as Amadou Diallo growing up.

JJ: Diallo was an African young man [23-year-old Guinean student] who was standing in his vestibule in the Bronx... [he was killed in 1999 by] undercover NYPD [plain-clothes officers: Sean Carroll, Richard Murphy, Edward McMellon, and Kenneth Boss, members of the "street Crime Unit" known for its brutality] – they give them a new name every two years after a scandal.

They rolled up on him. He had his wallet. Police said "It was a gun" and shot at him 41 times. Later, musician Bruce Springsteen wrote/performed the song *American Skin (41 Shots)*. This is when Rudolph Giuliani was New York City mayor before he became a global brand for militarized policing, exporting it to other countries, and aligned with [President Donald] Trump.

That killing, execution shocked New Yorkers. In 2014, Eric Garner was choked to death; Mike Brown was shot in Ferguson Missouri by police officer Darren Wilson and [the 18-year-old's] body was left on the ground for four hours; and, Tamir Rice, the twelve-year-old son of Samaria Rice, was shot by Timothy Loehmann, still another white police officer, in Ohio. This wave of police brutality, police killings dishonor became a catalyst [for people to see clearly the violence of] anti-Black policing. Did these deaths become a catalyst for the way you began to look at politics?

FC: For sure. I think coming up in Mayor Rudy Giuliani's New York [had an impact on me]. We talk about the vast colonial structure that exists in this country. Go back to the first year when [progressive Black former Mayor David] Dinkins loses; and [NYPD Commissioner Bill] Bratton and Giuliani come in together. At the same time, [in the 1990s, Professor Emeritus of Criminal Justice, Andrew Young School of Policy Studies] Robbie Friedman – who runs the GILEE [Georgia International Law Enforcement Exchange] program at Georgia State University – is writing tracts about broken windows policing and distributing this in the academic world.

All of these ideas are developing and you came up in what a lot of people consider to be the last interesting time to be in New York City, and suddenly saw it shift into this apartheid shopping center that Manhattan sort of became overnight. You recognize your own complicity in that system just by virtue of your birth and your actions, my actions, and to understand which I did by then, that everything I've ever benefited from comes off the backs of the workers of the country broadly, especially of colonized

48

people, whether they came from Africa or whether they came from a million other countries or whether they lived here in the first place, and specifically from Georgia in the case of my family.

After a particularly useless period of my life, I felt compelled to dive in long term. Occupy is the one thing that happened after the death of the left after the Cold War, but Occupy [Wall Street, formed in 2011 against income inequality] has zero race consciousness, zero discussion about colonialism, white supremacy, and imperialism. But after 2011, there was Ferguson [2014 police killing of 18-year-old Michael Brown], Baltimore [2015 police killing of Freddie Gray], Standing Rock [2017 Indigenous/Lakota-led protests against the Dakota Access Pipeline for oil fields that would pollute ground water] in succession. I was there [at Standing Rock] for most of the winter encampment which created a new discussion that helped reconstruct the foundation of a serious left in the North Atlantic sphere. I guess I got swept into that [early resistance] luckily in Atlanta.

KC: A young man [26-year-old bipolar, Black Air Force veteran with PTSD] ... totally naked, was shot in the DeKalb County area: Anthony Hill. It's a damn shame. The cop [Robert Olsen was sentenced in 2019 to 20 years but to serve 12; his conviction was overturned in March 2024]. Hill was having a mental health episode in broad daylight, totally unarmed. And this pig shot him twice, center mass. Hill didn't even have a wallet. He was a nude Black man and the cop felt "threatened." [Olsen told first responders that Hill had attacked him but video evidence and eyewitness contradicted his lies.] How would you define Cop City and your family's role in Cop City?

FC: I see Cop City as a training facility for probably various experimental and brutal forms of ruling-class terrorism. In the South End of Atlanta, in southwest Atlanta, specifically white supremacist terrorism, and gentrification, but also everywhere exist. As you said, this GILEE program is shuffling cops from Israel to narcos [illegal drugs/traffickers] in Honduras. We also know that Atlanta is not very far behind London in terms of being the city with the most police surveillance in the world. It is in the top five on that list right now.

Our family gave away a building that the newspaper once operated in, the *Atlanta Journal-Constitution*, which we still own and we still run. There was a building downtown that the paper had been in; don't hit me with slander, I'm going to say "I'm not sure," but I believe the city converted that building to act as a police surveillance training site, like sort of cybersecurity training. We do have involvement in cloud technology with the DOD [Department of Defense], although we're not particularly in that field. So, it's just like the pervasiveness of police violence in any white corporate structures now, it's beyond what it ever was because I think we actually have far greater revolutionary conditions than we had 20 years ago. Even white liberal people in charge who used to be more performatively anti-cop, are less so outwardly anti-police than they used to be.

KC: Your family owns the *Atlanta Journal-Constitution* – a heavy piece of propaganda when it comes to imperialism. Tell us about your family.

FC: My family is the Cox family. I think most family members have that name somewhere in their middle name. My great-grandfather was a governor of Ohio and started a media company. It became a major media company. Traditional newspapers, radio stations, and TV are not making a lot of money these days; but around the 1990s or so, we switched most of our investments into automotive and then cable and internet. So, now in terms of the force that we bring to the table on a material level, we're one of the largest cable internet providers in the country, and we own the largest wholesale auto auction business in the world, which is called Manheim Auto Auctions; and we own Auto Trader and Kelley Blue Book and a whole bunch of the auto industry.

We have investments in God knows what, but we're also completely privately owned by my family. So, you can't buy stock in Cox on the market. We have investments in things, like some electric car company that we're shareholders in, but in terms of the actual Cox companies, we own the whole thing or... Well, I don't anymore as of a week ago, but the way it was structured, everybody was born into [the company] no matter what, and they were so obsessed with maintaining that dynastic control of the company that there wasn't really any way to get anyone out of it either, not easily.

I didn't grow up with that family. We're involved in everything in Atlanta. Because of this private ownership, when you think about a big media or just a big conglomerate, you think about CEOs making a lot of money, but maybe they own like 20 percent of the company and have a controlling share of voting stock. They don't have 100 percent control of the company. So, my family also became, from what I understand, the wealthiest collective family in Georgia pretty much for all of the last 50 to 60 years. In terms of the wealthiest families in the country, we're always in the top ten, so a bunch of billionaires in terms of

51

the generation that owns things, which is now my father's generation and above.

We still control a lot of media, whether it's lucrative or not, and we certainly control pretty much all of the bourgeois media in Atlanta, WSB-TV being the largest radio and TV affiliates, the *AJC* (*Atlanta Journal-Constitution*) being the paper of record. We have a strange relationship in which there's an independent reporter trying to dig up information on the NPR affiliates in Georgia.

Nothing gets said in Atlanta that we aren't okay with. We also developed a really strong relationship with the Black comprador class, the downtown bourgeoisie in Atlanta. This goes back as far as my grandmother who was bankrolling people like [former civil rights activist and former U.S. Ambassador] Andy Young and [the late congressman] John Lewis and my father picking up that torch with [US Senator Raphael] Warnock... You have this circuit of visible leaders in the Black bourgeoisie who are working in concert with the white corporate class that surrounds the affluent suburbs or parts of the city.

And that's the "Atlanta way" people refer to, a sort of capitalism and imperialism by proxy. We've related to that through our family foundation donating more than anyone, except the Coca-Cola Foundation, to the Atlanta Police Foundation (APF). State Farm Arena Group, which my father is a member of the ownership group of the Atlanta Hawks and the arena, have donated millions. All of the other Atlantic corporations on whose boards people from Cox sit and vice versa have made donations to this thing. My cousin, who is the CEO of the company, claims it's an honorary rotating position, but he has been or had been sitting as the chair of the Atlanta Police Foundation.

Apparently, whoever's on the board, there's a rotating position, but this is all happening at the same time. This project is unfolding that we're caping for in the paper – giving the mayor an editorial, coming out as an editorial board in support of it, having him sit as the random honorary chair, giving it ten million. There's a lot going on here, and we have these connections to the military police industrial complex.

JJ: So, Noam Chomsky and Edward Herman could have written a book on your father and your family in terms of media, and "manufacturing consent." How do you see organizing encountering these mega productions that shape reality. People know that Tortuguita was shot 57 times, but the horror doesn't really hit some because the narrative, especially NPR, can influence us to remain in alignment with the *New York Times*. There's clutch the pearls outrage: "Oh, blood, death!" "Oh, that's so messy!" But mass media keeps churning out the same narrative: obey the law, follow the state, be a "good citizen." How do you see the alternative, the left, the radical journalists, theorists, podcasters putting a dent into that?

FC: I think specifically in the ideological sphere, if that's what you're asking because I think there are different answers and different tactics depending on what level you're operating on. In my limited forays into journalism, I've tried to put myself in positions that I can afford to put myself into in order to talk about what our traditional media sources won't talk about.

I think it's important for us at large to be developing revolutionary institutions and revolutionary infrastructure because they have thinktanks and research institutes that we don't. So, there's a couple of generations that are lacking context. So, when they come with correct political instinct, they don't know where to go with it. So, it goes into nothingness or it goes to the right wing or liberal organizing under the umbrella of NGOs (non-governmental organizations). On the ideological level, I'm interested in developing actual media that recognizes that there's no such thing as unbiased media.

I think coordination is really important, whatever that United Front looks like. There are anarchists, Marxist-Leninists, Black nationalists, liberals, and sort of like eco-liberals that are dedicated to that Cop City struggle and not in a way that's opportunistic, creating too big of a tent, and pretending that we are friends with someone more than we are.

KC: A functional unity type situation? How has your family accepted your brand of politics? How does that work for you?

FC: I don't have a relationship with anyone in my father's family. I did with my grandmother, I did with my father for some time, not really with others.... .

JJ: Cox is a multi-billion-dollar corporation, but the clergy – the Catholic Church has real money – and the churches function as machines of accumulation, as noted in Reverend Matt Johnson's "Letter of Concern to Black Clergy Regarding Cop City." Both Johnson and Chambers are rebelling against institutions that are incredibly powerful and that control messaging. How do you all see this struggle that you are waging against behemoths?

Reverend Matthew Johnson (MJ): Kalonji, Dr. James, thank you for having me. Fergie, I appreciate the support that you've given our folks. Outward opposition, you'll virtually never see any white people, and this is very intentional. The city of Atlanta has been brilliant at the identity politics game that they just turn into a lead capture. Specifically, they lean on the legacy of Rev. Martin Luther King as a tabula rasa for whatever the hell Black leadership chooses to do to secure their own position at the expense of the Black masses in Atlanta. One of the ways they do this is by having clergy on hand that are easily bought and sold for pennies on the dollar. Everybody else stands to gain from the policy decisions that they blindly accept with virtually no knowledge or with a pocketful of money.

After I wrote the "A Letter of Concern to Black Clergy" (see Chapter 3), in March, a friend found that Gerald Durley, who was on the advisory committee for Cop City, received $10,000 from the city for his birthday alone. They have gotten so used to being corrupt that people left it on plain paper. If you look at the first [promotional] commercial, Cop City was initially called the Institute for Social Justice. They put Martin Luther King and The King Center in the initial commercial promos saying that this was an extension of King's fight for a more perfect union and justice. This was utterly shameless from the beginning. There is a part of me that laughs to stop from crying... Raphael Warnock [is] preaching from the same pulpit as Martin Luther King Jr., hosting a vigil for George Floyd, and the funeral for Rayshard Brooks [both Black men killed by police]. As soon as Warnock gets in office [as a U.S. Senator from Georgia], he's beating the drum for his second [electoral] campaign. He is talking about the strength of the military because [corporate] outposts such as [weapons manufacturer] Lockheed Martin employ Georgians.

These people use rhetoric of "new, stronger leadership that we can trust" [as] moral stances; but they're really selling stances to the highest bidder. We've seen Raphael Warnock be absolutely mute at best about the Cop City project. We've seen this with the Concerned Black Clergy. These people only seem to get concerned after an open showing of property destruction, not when nonviolent protesters were being dragged out of the forest in dozens. They weren't concerned when somebody [Tortuguita] got murdered, and we all knew it was a cover-up. They got concerned when somebody told them that they needed to be concerned. I think that we're just so tired of business as usual. Atlantans are hurting too bad. When it comes to the wealth disparity, it's gotten worse. It's set a record every year since 2018, and now for every $1 of the Black median household income, it's $3 for the white median household income in Atlanta.

You'll have people that are still trying to put forward this idea that Black folks can galvanize behind with this "Black Mecca" idea; but only 5 percent of us are making it out of poverty. Too many people have seen the same thing from decade to decade to keep buying this bullshit.

I'm really glad that we've had more out-front clergy folks and Black organizers speaking truth to these issues. A lot of people, especially this bourgeois/political class of Black folks, have stepped back because they don't want to be in conflict with people that are genuine.

You can pull this game and maybe get a couple of news clips... but when you have very active opposition engaging in a language that folks understand – you can't continue to marginalize the Cop City opposition as being a couple of white folks that just hang out in the forest. We call on these particular clergy every time there's a problem, and they never point to any systemic injustices with any intention of changing them.

KC: Raphael Warnock organized with us around the Troy Davis campaign [Davis was executed in 2011 for a killing that he and his supporters, including the Pope, insisted he did not commit; no material evidence indicated his guilt]. We held a number of demonstrations at his church.

Whenever anything major was happening, we'd be marching from the state capitol to Ebenezer Baptist Church (Martin Luther King's old church). When the election happened, Warnock was already pegged as an "activist" [who was] taking on King's legacy. When you talk about people like Gerald Durley, you're not talking about just a pastor, but [also] power brokers.

Atlanta is one of the [key] homes of the megachurch, not necessarily in building and size, but in capacity. When Fergie talked about the Black bourgeois class and these gatekeepers, the church is the first line of defense here in Georgia. The entertainers and the church, they're side-by-side. From film director/entertainer Tyler Perry to deceased pastor of a Baptist megachurch Eddie Long – it is the same gang. What is this letter you wrote to the Black clergy?

MJ: I moved back to Georgia in 2019. Before seminary, I spent three years primarily in Sub-Saharan Africa, working on foreign direct investment reports (which we all kind of knew were bullshit in Sub-Saharan countries). We interviewed the CEOs of companies and ministers of government. Most of the countries I was working in had post-socialist links. In Ghana, I [met] people with connections to the CPP [Convention People's Party formed in 1949 led by President Kwame Nkrumah].

So, I came in with a different consciousness, but I jumped through all the hoops. I went to Morehouse, then to the University of Chicago, and followed their rules. So, there are certain ways that they can't say I'm out of left field. I had seen how disingenuous many of the preachers were when pressed. I just sat back watching, waiting. If I saw somebody doing something good, [I thought] "Okay, I can help."

I attended Rayshard Brooks's funeral hosted by Reverend Warnock. I reached out to [Warnock] when I had first gotten back into town. I just kept watching. What I saw was people using dead Black bodies as props when it was convenient, but not willing to make any strong stances when they had the power. So, if I'm watching you for a couple of years and you have all the quippy things to say when police are arrested, but now you are in the U.S. Senate and have nothing [material] to say? It's sketchy. People worked like hell to get into positions of esteem and proximity to power, but once they got there, it was mission accomplished for them and their prophetic voice went mute.

Everybody doesn't believe in God. Fine. But if you've made yourself the mouthpiece of the biggest entity in the entire cosmos by saying that you're a preacher on behalf of this ultimate being, and you do it for your own benefit – I have no respect for that…

When you have a preacher in the midst, they'll always jump out-front first, but the first ones to try to negotiate with somebody [from the state/corporation], and that is never a model for solidarity. Essentially white policy always uses Black intelligentsia, the political class, and religious establishments for cover.

One thing that I heard when I was much younger is "You will never go broke telling white people what they want to hear." I had tried to touch base with Gerald Durley the week before but he said that he was very busy. So, to see this 80+ year old man Durley get on stage a week later to condemn protesters with nothing else to say about the Cop City project was, in one way, a slap in the face. But it was also a very clear realization of these people's roles. They continue to sell out working-class interests.

It was the Friday week of action [March 10], shortly after it was announced that there were at least a dozen gunshot wounds found on Tortuguita's body with no evidentiary significance that Tortuguita fired back as they had their hands up. That was the same day as the first press conference with the Concerned Black clergy. Atlanta Mayor Andre Dickens follows up in mid-April with another press conference where he has at least 50 Black folks behind him, most of them men, virtually nobody white in the background, leaning on images of the well-to-do Black bourgeoisie.

Just a couple hours later, media and activists announced that there were more than 50 gunshot wounds on Tortuguita's body and no gunshot residue that would indicate that they shot first… Atlanta literally used Black bodies as cover for what they knew was damn corrupt, twice in those press conferences, obscuring details about a murder.

MJ: Three dozen people had their lives changed forever because of the association with "domestic terrorism" without a shred of evidence. To watch city council members say, "Well, I don't know what to tell you. I hope it doesn't happen to you," as they're voting to support Cop City after they just arrested a bail fund [activist] (with them saying on radio that it was a part of a political repression move). I can't associate with this apparatus.

JJ: The three of you [Changa, Johnson, Chambers] bring to my mind the United Front Against Fascism. Fergie mentioned them earlier. But also other people [have raised the concept] such as Panther veteran Dhoruba bin-Wahad, and Chairman Mao's statement [June 23, 1941, "On the International United Front Against Fascism"] when the Nazis invaded Soviet territory. The U.S. COINTEL-PRO, which is lethal and murderous, [is an example of "fascist policing."] The Cop City project is [about] class/race war. Opposition to fascist formations requires international thinking. Nahel Merzouk [https://theintercept.com/2023/07/12/france-riots-police-nahel-merzouk/], a seventeen-year-old in France, was killed by militarized police in July 2023 [which sparked mass protests]. What does the United Front Against Fascism look like to you?

FC: Well, we just covered [General Secretary of the Bulgarian Communist Party, 1946–1949] Georgi Dimitrov's work on the United Front against Fascism in our study group; and now we're reading George Jackson [slain imprisoned revolutionary, author of *Soledad Brother* and *Blood in My Eye*]. It's a matter of identifying these moments where we see fascism consolidating itself, and noting the primary contradictions that we're facing internationally and domestically.

In the United States, we know our engagement in imperialism abroad is deeply interconnected with police violence here [domestically] in the colonization of our own neighborhoods. and the people who live here. We need to get organized. Joining explicitly radical, political organizations, revolutionary organizations that have correct lines on those primary points of contradiction (being police violence, the carceral system, anti-imperialist struggle globally). COINTELPRO, which was cited earlier, was incredibly effective at fracturing and compartmentalizing all the elements of the left (when there was a real left), with revolutionary potential that had a generation of educated cadre.

That pressure, as Matthew pointed out, is coming down on some of the left political class in Georgia. Senators Ossoff and Warnock had to make these milquetoast statements that didn't mean anything, but it moved them in a way. The fact that so many people even know about a facility like this being built in Georgia is reflective of that. This is the process through which power is built, and there are people who have survived in the vacuum of the '90s and the 2000s who were revolutionary leaders and never took that white-blood money. Some of them maybe got out of prison and a lot of them are in prison, but some of that legacy has existed and filtered its way into this generation.

KC: This is money coming off the blood of the people. If we say "white money," we don't want to confuse people into thinking that somehow this was some type of legitimate capitalist, "pull yourself up by the bootstrap" endeavor. This is literally the blood and sacrifice of millions of people across the globe... definitely I unite with what you're saying. Matthew, your take on the United Front Against Fascism?

MJ: A lot of this is internal. We should always be coming to the table knowing that our ideologies are supposed to be a practice and used for praxis rather than them being our standing identity. If you're coming to the table already thinking about yourself as an anarchist or anti-racist or as a male feminist, etc., and you look at that as your fixed identity – when somebody calls you on it, rather than looking at it as an opportunity to grow, you see it as an attack on who you are as a person. This is important, especially when you're coming with people that might naturally have more skin in the game or coming from different identities that aren't as well represented....

When people are saying, "Hey, this is an issue!" Rather than being defensive, say "Okay, well maybe I don't see the whole picture and we need to grow from there." This type of reflexive building with one another is key for us organizing in a new way and creating a new world as we go along.

When it comes to having a United Front, being able to keep those channels of dialogue open is essential. I was reading *Elite Capture* by Olufemi Taiwo, they explain the initial presence of identity politics in spaces. It was meant for people to bring their own community's particular issues to the table from their own experience – what people were suffering with as an opportunity to expand our consciousness and see how things are interrelated.

So, when we're going into city hall to make a big demonstration and somebody else is talking about the shutting down of different stops on the MARTA (Metropolitan Atlanta Rapid Transit Authority), and someone else is talking about rent control it's important to be able to have these conversations in context. Norfolk Southern Railway corporation spent $1 million on Cop City, the corporation also ensured that workers couldn't strike when they were saying that trains were understaffed and unsafe. These aren't just one-off issues – transportation was packaged as a security issue. People did not feel safe going to these

MARTA stops and that is why they shut them down. [Police were/are] protecting this facility that nobody wants with this Cop City facility, you just got more and more cops to protect corporate property. Ask yourself: "Do the cops really keep us safer?" Shit, aren't you as scared as you were 30 years ago? We've lost a lot of our kids, where are they at?

KC: Matthew is my kind of preacher for cops.

JJ: Thank you, Matt and Fergie. This is very enlightening and courageous. Stay well, and courage and spirit to you all.

KC: Yes, in the words of George Jackson, "We will never be counted amongst the broken men."

JJ: Or, [broken] women, and non-binary people.

KC: I love that. We'll catch you all in the whirlwind.

CHAPTER FIVE

Tortuguita's Mother Speaks: Belkis Terán

BPM/RSTV Interview with Kalonji Changa, January 2024

Kalonji Changa (KC): Today, we commemorate the eve of the cold-blooded murder of Manuel Esteban Páez-Terán, known to many of us here in the Atlanta area as "Tortuguita." They were a young environmental activist, an eco-Anarchist, who was shot and killed by the Georgia State Patrol. Georgia State Patrol later claimed that they fired on them, but those charges are false. Tortuguita was shot 57 times, 57 gunshot wounds, no visible gunpowder residue was found on their hands. Their hands were up and yet the police murdered them; and no one was charged. Today, we wanted to bring in a relative of Tortuguita, the mother, Belkis, who is visiting Atlanta and agreed to come on RSTV on this one-year anniversary [of the murder of her child]. Belkis, how are you doing today?

Belkis Terán (BT): Good. Thank you. I feel very honored to be here. Thank you very much for this opportunity.

KC: We are honored to have you. We know that it hasn't been easy for you. Thank you [for being here] and for raising a great child. If you don't mind sharing with us, who is and who was Tortuguita to you?

BT: Tortuguita, Tort, Manuel is my second child. All their life, they were very intense, very charismatic. They fulfilled everything since they were born. I named them Manuel because they come from Emmanuel. That means "God" to us. I raised them in a very Christian tradition. I was not very religious. But we followed Biblical principles. I always told my children the principle of life is that we have to respect and consider each other. Based on Jesus's word that you must love your neighbor as yourself, I think this is the most powerful law in the universe. That love helps everybody grow and give the best of yourself.

Manuel, Tort, Tortuguita grew up in a very healthy way, being attentive and traveling to different countries. They studied in Aruba, England, Egypt, Houston, the United States, Russia. We are a family with a very open cosmosvisional life. We are not rich, but [we have] the possibility to have all these experiences. Early on, they [Tortuguita] showed an interest in connecting with other people. When it was Christmas time, I saw them give their presents to other children. I said, "Manuel, no, don't do that. This is yours." They responded: "Mami, but the boy doesn't have a toy. I like him to have a toy," they said. I replied "Yes, but this is for you." So, I managed to give them other toys, saying: "Okay, we can give them this toy and you keep your own." All their life, they were selfless. Similarly, when they were working two, three years ago, they gave away $2,000 to other people. Exactly the same conversations. I said, "Manuel, why are you giving your money away?" They said: "Mami, I don't need it. These people need it."

They made a very deep impact in the community. They were very intense, very active with so many people. They helped so many people. [People would come to me and say,] "Oh, your child did this for me." And, I'm amazed.

The way that they killed him, it was very horrible. I don't have the words. There were 57 wounds in his body. Some of those wounds [were] with one bullet, [others with] four. Four wounds [made with] one bullet. I was devastated about that; how could they massacre a person alone in the forest? They [police] are supposed to protect, not to kill people in the forest. But this investigation is done by lawyers. The police are making their own assumptions, and they believe that they have the truth. I don't believe them. So, we are working on that.

KC: When you got this news, I am sure that it was a moment in your life that you will never forget. Where were you? Did someone call you?

BT: One of the forest defenders – she was from the plant in Tallahassee where Manuel was for a few years. I met a lot of his friends there. The day after they were killed I got a message. She is one of my daughters now, and she said, "I am sorry about Mani, and you are a great mother. You raised a gentle soul. I'm sorry about that." I was in Panama, so I said, "What are you talking about?" She sent me the news links, and I said, "Wow."

I am a person that doesn't react immediately. I'm very slow to react. So, I investigated. I called their father. I called my son. We started to investigate. The first thing that [was] said is that Tortuguita shot the police. I think "How?" How could that happen? The other thing I saw [in the media claim] was that Tortuguita was running away from the police. But we later discovered that Tortuguita was sitting with their hands up. So yeah, it was very painful. It is painful. I just finished crying a few minutes ago. I mean, I can be strong, but I know it's going to be very hard today, tomorrow, and all this week. I'm trying to have my tea and breathe, because it's going to be hard. I like to be strong because I have a message to give. I raised a person that is a big light, big heart. Love. I grew up with a lot of love. My relationship with Manuel was like this. We told everything to each other. And when they decided in May 2022 to go to the forest defender, they sent me a picture with their gear and stated: "I'm going to be taking courses to be doctor, a street doctor." They already did this training in Aruba, Panama, and Atlanta. In Panama, they attended Florida State University [originated in Panama in 1957, parent campus is Tallahassee, Florida]. They created the environmental club together with their friends.

Tortuguita was an activist before they arrived to the United States, cleaning beaches, working, helping. On the weekends, they went to the park to take care of the old people, bringing water to them in their wheelchairs. They were active. I plan to do the same. I plan to continue doing something, not only protest. Protest is important, but we have to change our ways of being. We have to spend more time doing something for the community, instead of watching TV or playing games or being by yourself. There are so many things to do outside or for the community or for your neighbor. That it is part of what Jesus said to us. I was asking Manuel, "Why don't you go to church?" They said, "If I go to church, I'm going to be sitting in a chair listening about a bunch of things I already know, and I'm losing my time there. Better go outside and clean the beach or help. I don't think it's bad to [go to church], but for me, I prefer action. Go do this, do that." So, in the same way, instead of being in my room crying for them – I will do something. And that is why I created the "Tortuguita

Healing Center," which I want to be interactive. Then we can share ways to heal because I don't have all the answers.

Why healing? Because Tortuguita is not here anymore. We need to be good inside. Then we can open and connect with people from our light. If we connect with people from our anger, from our sorrow, from our cry, from our sadness, the connection is not going to be as positive as it could be. But if we connect from our light, from our love, then we can make positive [changes] for our community and we can change the world. I think the world needs to be changed. I think I'm now becoming an abolitionist.

KC: That's a beautiful thing.

BT: Yes, I think there are a lot of institutions that must be abolished, but we have to create the movement. We have to create the environment to destroy those institutions that are a cancer to our society. The... drug people or the robbers or the killers in the society that are in jail or in prison without any opportunity to reform... are not the cancer. The cancer is the institution. The institution that doesn't provide help for those people, especially in the United States where a lot of people are suffering from emotional problems. Most of them try to solve their suffering through drugs. And sometimes the institutions create addictions for those people.

KC: Absolutely.

BT: I used to work as an alcoholism and drug abuse counselor in Chicago many years ago. I was in an institution that helped create this addiction to methadone. Instead of helping them get off the drugs... cocaine or whatever, they put these people in institutions to use methadone.

KC: Get them hooked on methadone.

BT: Without any real interest in cleaning the people from the drugs. So, you see how the system is. I was a counselor for 26 people. And in a year's time, I helped two people to get off the drugs. But all the counselors, they don't care. They are in the system and they just increase the methadone. I just get my salary and go home.

KC: It's important that you say that because the institution moves them from one addiction to the next. And like you said, this is what America does to you. They continue to criminalize and demonize. They lock someone up for some petty charges in the name of reform, but it's no real reform. It is more like, let's put you in this cage; it's a modern form of enslavement. I am glad you're sharing that part because for years we've been telling folks the methadone clinics are another form of addiction. It's like, let's take you off of these "illegal drugs" and let's put you on something that we sanction that we can make money off of.

BT: Methadone is more addictive than cocaine and any other drug on the street. And they know that. But money is the priority. Now with Cop City, it's the same. All this controversy, all this movement, trying to avoid the citizens. The people don't want a Cop City, but there is a lot of money and investment involved in the city.

KC: The mayor.

BT: They don't care. I see these governors. They own the cities. They act like the landlords of the city, and they are not because the city doesn't belong to them. It belongs to the people. But the government and large corporations don't listen because they have the power. So, the community has to organize themselves. The community has to slowly create links to heal themselves, and from the light, from the love, from the good ideas, transform the society from the bottom.

KC: Have any of these "elected officials" ever reached out to you? I know that you said you found out about Manuel's death through a friend 24 hours later. Did anyone from the Atlanta/Georgia government ever reach out to you to say, "Our condolences."

BT: No, never. Never, never, never.

KC: Not one person.

BT: No, no, no. We tried for a long time. Then we got connection with one later, but it was just after so much knocking doors and then one of, I don't want to say names or anything, but...

KC: You can feel free to do so.

BT: I don't remember.

KC: Okay.

BT: I know that one time I got the opportunity to talk to Atlanta City Council member Westmoreland, I think it was.

KC: The city councilman.

BT: We passed by and saw Mayor Andre Dickens there and someone said, "Oh, stop to talk to Dickens." Dickens never shows his face. But I talked to Matt Westmoreland, he said he is in favor of Cop City. Then we talked to City Council member Liliana Bakhtiari and she voted No against Cop City. But there were more votes for Cop City.

KC: When you heard the news reports that Tort had fired on the cops, what was your thought on that? Did you ever think that that was even possible? Because from what you're telling us, it sounds like this is a loving, giving person... someone that was raised to respect people.

BT: I thought it was a mistake. I thought that they were confusing Tortuguita for somebody else, but then I investigated. Because they said that Tort was in land that doesn't belong to them, that it was not accessible to people. But then we discovered that they were in a park, open to everybody. Well, I thought there was a mistake; they were looking to prove something. But they killed my child in cold blood. That's what I think. Because Manuel was sitting in the tent. Later on, I went to the Weelaunee Forest. It was not yet closed to the public. I collected things on the floor ground that I knew belonged to my child.

KC: How long after that murder did you visit?

71

BT: Fifteen days or three weeks later.

KC: Their belongings were still there?

BT: Yeah. They troopers made a mess. There were bullets all over the place. Holes in the clothes. The police were throwing everything on the floor. Really a mess. Emanuel was a very clean person who liked everything neat.

KC: Was this a tent?

BT: It was a tent.

KC: So, you could see the holes all through the tent?

BT: No, no, no. They took the tent, but I could see the suitcase. They had a suitcase full of bullets. I found bullets in a shoe. We saw holes in the trees. We saw one of Tortuguita's pants full of bullets and it was thrown on the floor. A lot of garbage. And we went there to collect all the garbage and throw everything in the garbage cans. There was a flute that they had there. I took it and more personal things – their suitcase, I left it there. Somebody was using it later. I don't know what happened with the suitcase and clothes. I left them because there were still good clothes that anybody can use.

KC: We know that Tortuguita was murdered in cold blood. No charges have been brought. The city pretty much disregarded you. We don't know how you would have found out that your child was even murdered if you hadn't gotten this message from their friend. What would you like to see done and what are your thoughts on Cop City as a whole?

BT: Well, I want to stop the construction of Cop City, but most of all, I want them to recognize what they did wrong. Manuel was not a threat to anybody. Lawyers are investigating. And they don't have it easy because everything is so mysterious. But they will continue looking for information and present something. We don't want to make assumptions now, just wait to see what can be done. So, for me, I am busy now, like I say, with this healing.

A lot of people in the forest defenders are wounded, are suffering. I think my position as a mother, as Tortuguita's mother, is to help those people to heal and continue life and continue programs. I like to continue and to support food programs/housing programs – not only in the United States, but in Panama. I am trying to do it in Panama too, because that was some of my advice to Manuel. I said, "Manuel, if it's so difficult in Atlanta, why don't you go to California? Go to the Muskogee land in Oklahoma? Why don't you go there?"

The world is so open for opportunities to serve. Even now, for example, with Palestine. Many people are helping in Palestine, protecting children, working on what they can save. And in Egypt, people are trying to help. The world is terrible, but as long as we can do something… Now there is protest. Protest so that people in power have to stop and allow people to rebuild their life. For actions like the war or actions that are far away from us, I just pray because I believe that we can send energy to the world to heal. Around us, in our neighborhoods, we can do things too. We have to build trees, and to continue building forests. Some women in India are rebuilding forest areas. There are actions that people are doing all over the world; and we can do it. The opportunities are there. Just you have to identify an action. My way is healing with oils, for example. I use essential oils. To relax, I use Ashwagandha an herb from Asia/Africa used for stress.

Go to the natural. We don't need to have cocaine. We don't need to have drugs. In this part of the world, we are busy with our lives and this system is very stressful. You need to pay taxes, you need to do this, you need to do that. So, take a moment for meditation. Take a moment for yourself. If you heal yourself, then you have more life to share. And this will immediately create opportunities. When you focus only on the bad things and you don't see the good things in your life, then you contaminate yourself. I know because you are a very protestor person, but I'm sure that you need to have your own equilibrium and you work on that. Because if you don't have your own equilibrium, you cannot continue. All this information kills you.

KC: What you are saying right now is right on time. I am so grateful. You remind me of another Belkis, another beautiful Belkis from tenth-century BC Ethiopia and Yemen. This Belkis also talks about: healing, meditation, herbs. Belkis an Arabic name means the queen of Sheba. So, not only did Manuel have a great name, you have a great name as well. And, that's good to know that you all are living those names out because oftentimes people take on names that they cannot fulfill.

I appreciate you sharing the healing modalities with our audience. And how can we assist as far as keeping the name "Tortuguita" alive and assisting in the healing aspects? How can we reach you?

BT: Well, what we can do is to plant trees, take care of nature in any way. Feed the poor, try to find the people that are in need around you and help to shelter people, too. There is now a big fight in the cities about gentrification because it takes all the people that cannot pay for a good place and makes them move away. Try to make a voice about that! Organize with your church. There are so many ways that we can connect with people. I know I have to be very careful. I always say: don't do anything alone. Get out of your television.

KC: That's the first stop. That and social media.

BT: Yeah, the television or the telephone is connecting you to here, but you have to connect here to outside. And this is healthy, to listen to programs like this [RSTV/BPM]. But you have to try to be with real people. That's why I want to see you in person and hold you.

KC: And you will. I know that you have a ton of things to do today, but I really appreciate you taking time out of your schedule here on the eve of the anniversary of your child's murder. But we say that they're not dead. Their spirit moved on and the work will move through, because just seeing you as a mother, we know that Tortuguita was not a victim… Tortuguita was victorious. The state killed their body, but their spirit and their name move on and live on. And the work that you're talking about will inspire many more.

BT: Manuel was inspiring. Tortuguita, they were inspiring. So, I like to share this with everybody: We need to rescue the earth. We need to get a higher vibration. Manuel is light right now. They are light. That's why I found my power. There is a legacy that we can follow. We have to continue their legacy, their work… from the light… not from anger, not from your problems but from the light.

KC: We will see you soon. Be safe out here. Let us know if you need anything. Thank you. We will win.[1]

Graduate Student poster for 2023 University of Michigan-Ann Arbor Conference on Insurgencies. Students organized postcard-writing for incarcerated environmentalists—arrested while attending a peaceful music festival—and asked keynote speaker James to visit forest protesters in Atlanta.

PART II

PART II

CHAPTER SIX

Combat Police Terror

Dhoruba bin Wahad and Kalonji Changa

National Coalition to Combat Police Terrorism

The National Coalition to Combat Police Terrorism (NCCPT) was conceived to address the foremost obstacle and institutional threat to freedom and democracy, community safety of working-class neighborhoods in America today. That is, generally speaking, a Police State masquerading as a "democracy" which views all Black and brown citizens as potential criminals. Techniques of Stop-and-Frisk, no knock invasions of private dwelling, arbitrary police brutality, and murder of Black people are all employed to instill fear of, and unquestioning obedience to, the armed agents of the State.

Add to this equation the historical white supremacist construct of America's economic and political system, Americans, especially those of African ancestry, are confronted with a corporate Police State and militarized policing that eagerly repress all political dissent not endorsed by the status quo and political elite, defining such dissent as terrorism, or supportive of terrorism. Consequently, enforcement of "Law and Order" by militarized police becomes anti-terrorism, when in fact the opposite is true. Public fear of state-sanctioned violence is a prerequisite for a social order that rely upon race and class for "equal treatment under the law."

Therefore, it is the purpose and mission of NCCPT to challenge the institutionalization of Racist Police Terror (RPT) and violence implemented under the color of law. To create mechanism of accountability for police misconduct and thwart the rise of right-wing, organized police fraternities that shield police misconduct from scrutiny and public accountability. Police fraternities posing as labor unions exert an inordinate amount of political influence over Black and progressive elected representatives, prosecutors, judges, and taxpayers.

Decertification and Recertification of Police Unions

To reform or rethink policing in America without a full appreciation and understanding of the actual danger militarized policing poses to a legitimate democracy is impossible. Meaningful reform of policing cannot be achieved without an appreciation that America is controlled by armed state agents posing as "civil servants" who are controlled by corporate donors but yet are funded by taxpayer dollars while remaining beyond public accountability. Police "unions" are the primary conduits of corporate contributions to the police. Consequently, police accountability to the taxpayer is thwarted by the contrived political influence of well-funded police unions which politically reinforce insular "police culture" and institutional racism that protects violent-prone policing and racial profiling. This all operates despite a Black police chief or Black mayor, who more often than not provides cover for rogue police units and departments.

The American public must be educated to the threat posed to democracy by this burgeoning right-wing power of the police that draws its legitimacy from "fear of crime" (real and imagined) while corporations subsidize their military training. The creation of "Cop Cities" are manifestations of this arrangement. The "fear of crime" is the socio-political cover for "public safety," a mantra inter-changeable with "law and order." Police "reform" is an undertaking that will never effectively empower America's multi-racial working class without the demilitarization of law enforcement, that is, without reigning in the political power of armed agents of the State. This requires multi-organizational coalitions and ultimately "A National United Front Against the Corporate Military Police State" – and a third political party challenging the duopoly political party system.

Class-Action Initiatives

Progressive forces in America and anti-racist activists must rise up and confront the growing threat to what remains of "democracy" in America. Toward this end, a strategy of mass education regarding the true character and purpose of policing in particular and the terrorism deployed by out-of-control police departments that intimidate and terrorize the working-class poor under the color of law must be initiated. American "democratic fascism" is a reality that no longer can be dismissed and pigeonholed as "anti-police," "woke" militancy. Without the complicity of the police, the corporate-funded right-wing political rule by the rich in the United States cannot be effectively implemented and full-blown fascism institutionalized. Without citizen control of public safety, decentralization of militarized police departments, and genuine protection from police abuse and misconduct targeting the working class, Black people in particular, then everyone is subject to police murder, abuse, and brutality at any given moment.

Police in the United States "serve" the interests of the rich and "protect" the private property of America's corporate oligarchy. Police have no mandate to protect the working class, or uphold fair and equitable treatment of ordinary people. Indeed, the police in America believe that the public is subject to them and work for them not the reverse. Given this Orwellian scenario all sectors of the working poor, the marginalized and despised must combine forces to rein in police abuse, brutality, and murder under color of law. The state has a legal monopoly on violence and the police are their armed agents, while ordinary citizens have little or no protection against state-sanctioned violence, legal or otherwise.

The Rise of Right-Wing "Democratic Fascism" in the U.S. and Abroad

U.S. police exercise inordinate political power and exert considerable undemocratic influence over working-class communities and their elected state and municipal representatives through their certified "workers" unions which are not prohibited from receiving corporate or private funding. Police unions are *not* prohibited from influencing elected representatives and intimidating lawmakers outside the districts of their constituents' membership because the police are assumed to be workers when, in fact, they are armed agents of the State endowed with the power to arrest, detain, and even kill ordinary citizens.

Unlike the U.S. military that is ostensibly under civilian control and prohibited from entering into domestic partisan politics, the police – who are equally armed agents of the U.S. – have circumvented civilian control over their actions through the use of organized unions under the misappropriation of their status as "workers," and illogically considered mere "civil servants" of which they are effectively neither. The institutional device is the police unions.

Placing Police Power under Civilian Control

Police unions should be subject to special legitimate union certification that reflects their status as non-working-class armed agents of the State. They should be recertified to reflect their status as *armed civil servants*, with a code of conduct similar to the military's code of conduct, with prohibitions from participation in partisan politics as a union. To launch an educational initiative reformers, activists, and progressives alike should unify to immediately effectuate challenges to the Military-Police Law Enforcement Industry (MPLEI). In order to alert the working poor to the inordinate threat of police power, a class action civil litigation demanding the "decertification of police unions" is the first viable and purposeful legal strategy available.

Such a civil class action must draw a clear demarcation line between "legal reform" and the rights of working people to unionize. First, it must be noted that the police in the United States are first and foremost certified "armed agents of the state" and civil employees with powers and authority to enforce and regulate law enforcement; they also have the authority to kill, maim, and detain any citizen who in their estimation is breaking the law or about to break the law (probable cause). Police are also empowered to protect private property and the lives of ordinary citizens from criminal predation and crime. No other segment of the working class and their unions are endowed with such powers under the color of law.

We should enlist lawyers from civil rights formations, such as the Center for Constitutional Rights (CCR), NAACP Legal Defense Fund, National Council of Black Lawyers (NCBL), National Lawyers Guild (NGL) to form a legal ad hoc committee to bring *a class action lawsuit challenging police union certification. Seeking the abolishment of unconstitutional law enforcement privileges protected by police unions and seeking statutory relief:*

- Abolish qualified immunity.
- Strike down prohibitions that protect armed state agents from civil asset forfeiture.
- Eliminate union protections that require internal investigations without oversight.
- Make it a crime to mute or turn off cop body cameras.

Decertification of police unions and their recertification must at a minimum make it easy and cheap for citizens to get evidence of police misconduct, criminal activity under the color of law, and to review police administrative practices that encourage or sanction racial discrimination, racial profiling, religious/anti-Muslim discrimination, anti-poor/working-class status, and citizenship status. Civil defendants identified for a class action police union decertification should include the five largest U.S. police unions: Police Benevolent Association (PBA); Fraternal Order of Police (FOP); Chicago Police Unions; Los Angeles Police Unions; Atlanta Police Unions.

(The National Coalition to Combat Police Terrorism [NCCPT] was established in 2015 by veteran Black

Panther Party leader Dhoruba Bin Wahad, former U.S. Congresswoman Cynthia McKinney and FTP Movement founder Kalonji Jama Changa.)

The Strategic Safety Plan: A Future for Local Community Control

Given the events in the U.S. to defund and disband police departments, police *reforms* are not a solution for our liberation. They create opportunities for police killings, abuse and unaccountable police unions, which only cause further harm to our people. We've seen it. You've seen it. They must be abolished now!

The goal is to abolish the institution of policing and establish the complete autonomous community control of our public safety. We must continue to call for this reality. How do we get there? Tactics. Key tactics serve as escalation steps towards a larger strategy in a framework to abolish the institution of policing. These tactics work in order *and* together to bring us closer to our goal:

- Defund the police.
- Divest from the police.
- Disband the police.
- Decentralize the police.
- Establish community control of public safety.

Reforms that create vulnerabilities for police killings (e.g. community policing and increased training) and abuse (e.g. mandatory body cameras for all police officers) can exist but also undermine abolitionist strategies if we do not escalate our tactics. When we discuss solutions about disbanding departments, we are very clear about our stance on community control. The media has been using Camden, NJ, as an example of what disbanding the police looks like, but this is incorrect. Camden supposedly "consulted" with the community and then proceeded to impose reforms on their police department. The result was a county-operated police force that only exists because of fiscal mismanagement and failure to delegate power to the community. In other words, there was no disbandment; there was a re-formation of police and a reinstituting of policing. This distinction is very important and should not be conflated with abolishing and creating alternative modalities to the current institution of policing in poor, middle-class, and predominantly Black districts.

Policing reforms do not elicit any *substantial, permanent* consequences to police violence. To reimagine policing and public safety means to build policing and public safety in the name of community protection that is based on each community's socio-political interests, values, principles, culture and politics. This is why escalation tactics are necessary. We can no longer be occupied and distracted by policing reforms that we know do not work for us but maintain white supremacy, implicit bias.

Institutionalized police union politics and endemic racism continue to unleash a sustained anti-Black U.S. state-sponsored terrorism against Black domestic colonial-like enclaves, Bantustans, ghettoes, and urban slums. The solution to police misconduct, brutality, and murder inside Black, brown, and oppressed communities has existed for decades; however, it has largely been ignored. The brilliant strategy map developed by veterans of the "original" Young Lords, Black Panther Party, and Black Liberation Army offers an example of structure that could be realized in the largest U.S. police-occupied urban "territory" – New

86

York City. This outline was produced with the hope that concerned elected officials, lawyers, clergy, students, youth advocates, parents, educators, activists, and members of the media internationally will request, review, and respond to strategic safety plans developed and controlled by impacted communities.[1] As we all sincerely engage in critical dialog and organizing for *total* community control, *mandatory* police residency, and the *decentralization of urban forces* (such as the New York Police Department), we seek to *dismantle militarized "Cop Cities"* – scores of which are developing or already developed against U.S. residents.[2]

CHAPTER SEVEN

Assassination Attempts against Mumia Abu-Jamal

Pam Africa, Noel Hanrahan, Ricardo Alvarez, Kalonji Changa, and Joy James, GIU/BPM Interview, February 2024[1]

Kalonji Changa (KC): Peace good people. This is Guerilla Intellectual University (GIU), special edition. One of our favorite freedom fighters is in a crisis. He's been in crisis for over 40 years, we know that. We want to give an update on this crisis. I want to bring on my co-host, Dr. Joy James.

Joy James (JJ): I think we should rename GIU "Guerilla Intellectual *Union*," particularly because of the three guests today given their ability to work collectively under crisis, and also for a beloved. The union is more important than any stamp of university learning. GIU is an educational endeavor, but our commitments to each other are really the foundational texts.

KC: Talk about our guests.

JJ: Their model of fighting, resisting, and loving? Resistance to war, to torture, to murder under the guise of "medical care" [really] medical neglect – that is embodied in Pam Africa, Ricardo Alvarez and Noel Hanrahan. Advocates for Mumia Abu Jamal (MAJ). Mumia is a teacher, so we could call ourselves a university. But MAJ is going to be the head scholar, right? He is teaching us about what it means to have compassion, what it means to fight for our rights and our liberation, and to fight against a predatory state. He is also teaching how to love ourselves and link our intellect or advocacy into a fortress. This, Mumia has shown with light and love...

KJ: We have on GIU the founder of the International Concerned Family and Friends of Mumia Abu-Jamal, Pam Africa; Dr. Ricardo Alvarez, physician to Mumia; the founder of Prison Radio, attorney Noel Hanrahan. Good to have you all please share your updates on Mumia.

Noel Hanrahan (NH): Mumia Abu Jamal has been in prison now for 42 years. He survived three execution attempts: one on the streets of Philadelphia in 1981, and two literal execution warrants. It has been a real struggle for Mumia to communicate with us and to maintain his health. In the last eight years, Mumia has had many health struggles. We as a community have rallied to make sure that Mumia Abu Jamal has survived, just like we rallied when he was under an execution warrant.

He had severe hepatitis C, which there was a cure for but the prison was preventing him from getting medicine... mobilization literally made sure that Mumia was given that life-saving cure in 2017. Then he had double bypass heart surgery in 2021. He is suffering from a number of medical conditions.

Pam Africa (PA): Mumia has a tendency to not talk about himself, when he's damn near dying. He wanted to talk about other things, but there was no conversation to be had there except his deteriorating health. You know what he wants to talk about? His new book, *Beneath the Mountain: An Anti-Prison Reader.*[2]

Ricardo Alvarez (RA): I frame any discussion of a medical consultation with Mumia in the context of "What is torture"? A medical consultation with a brilliant public intellectual, a political prisoner... in prison by virtue of what he says, and not what he did... in this context, to do a medical consultation with Mumia in captivity means that there are nuances to words that he says that cue me into concern. One of the words he said, as it relates to the extent of his skin condition, is that it was "unstable." When Mumia was transferred out of the facility to see an outside cardiologist... he was shackled. He asked the prison guards, "Why am I shackled?" They said, "We don't know. We just know we're taking you to this place." He later said to me, "That's probably their protocol." He sees this cardiologist, and the cardiologist says to him: "Why are you here?" and suggests the shackles have increased his distress and health issues. Medical systems are so broken and stressful for all of the participants in that system. For patients, it's a hostile system; we literally describe doing community health work as being on the *front lines*, the sense of being on the front line [reflects] the *mindset of warfare*.

NH: They delayed Mumia's medical treatment for two years when they had the cure. And that delay increased his risk of having liver cancer, exacerbated his underlying conditions, including the skin condition, and extra hepatitis. Your skin is an organ. We went to court and got a third circuit injunction for Mumia to get the fast-acting cure for hepatitis C. That was allowed. That was used by other prisoners across the country. It was the first one. Mumia is one person, but we're advocating for everyone.

Mumia had double bypass surgery in 2021. They [the state/prison] have never provided him outpatient care; care for his diet and exercise which are the two key ingredients for recovering from cardiac surgery. He has been denied that now for over two years. That means he will likely have another cardiac event because they are denying him adequate care.

KC: Do you all feel that this is an assassination attempt of Mumia Abu-Jamal? There's medical neglect but I don't buy it that Mumia is just the average prisoner.

PA: No, he is not the average prisoner. And yes, they are definitely, and in front of our faces, attempting to kill Mumia, and all for the blood lust wishes of Maureen Faulkner, Officer Faulkner's widow, and the Fraternal Order of Police (FOP). The prison is in cahoots with it. Noel, remind them of the day in court that attorney Bob Boyle came across these papers; and, how we winded up in court dealing with the medical issues. The prison did not do right by Mumia, he filed grievances, and they turned them down.

RA: I've had challenging medical consultations all my life, but I will say that one of the blessings of being in relationship to such an expansive, spiritual being, is that Mumia draws in community: brilliant philosophers, brilliant historians, brilliant lawyers, brilliant humans and activists. Our capacity is impressive. I spoke to him about multidisciplinary struggle. Mumia said something to me that I will never forget: we need to have a memory that this has [state violence has] happened before [in order] to connect with the ancestors. We have to recall that there were examples where disciplines work together. We have to remember that the construction, the literal manifestation from its roots, hands, the construction of mass incarceration required multiple disciplines coming together. Architects, planners, medical systems, legal systems, corporate systems, [it] was multidisciplinary [violence] to put it together. We need to have *multidisciplinary* [efforts to] deconstruct, de-engineer the prison…

We're doing the work done by Laura Whitehorn and RAPP (Release Aging People in Prison) and others. The released elders have been a huge and powerful voice. There is a clear call: *"Liberate our elders, this is institutional elder abuse."*

RA: There is a sea change now in our multidisciplinary, professional society, to report elder abuse, if we can come together in a coordinated way, multidisciplinary unity, for mass incarceration abolition. If we can get a Mumia coalition together, and go to our professional societies and hold them accountable, then we can address the identified social determinants of health, specifically, the FOP [Fraternal Order of Police], in Mumia's case, and address the harms of unqualified immunity, right, or qualified immunity, that gives them permission. We can address those harms of the code of silence. We can identify corporations, an individual, Citizens United, and begin that process of doing a diagnostic analysis of their pathology, and bring that out into the public in concrete ways. Then we begin to create a coalition where we put correctly the culprit, the FOP, on trial. That's what I believe to be the next stage of struggle.

Our strategies are to keep Mumia alive, in transition to freedom immediately. If we can do that effectively, including the emerging ethical community, biomedical ethical community, with… consensus around abolitionist public health, working communication with the American Public Health Association, the AMA (American Medical Association). All of these institutions are filled with contradictions. No one is perfect here. Abolition is a humbling journey. But if we can begin that conversation in defense of our communities, I believe we will turn the tide, in effect, and honor the call, liberate our elders. And when we bring them back into our community, in a loving way, then they give us counsel on how to reverse engineer…

JJ: Thank you all for your courage and your consistency. What you describe reminds me of COINTELPRO. There are different ways to eliminate people. How do you see the strategy of resistance "war resistance" and "assassination resistance" when so much violence is obviously secreted. Prison is a fortress of pain, intimidation and death. You have to be able to get inside to get the narrative and… bring it out. What would you like us to do in terms of mobilization, and organizing on an international level? People across the globe support Mumia… What roles should we play in the effort to stop medical assassinations and harm within prison and beyond those walls?[3]

RA: One of Mumia's lessons that helps to expand an understanding of "Love Not Phear" is compassion. There is no monolithic medical prison community, we have to appreciate… When Mumia was hospitalized and we mobilized around the four-point shackling when he shared that trauma. Imagine being in four-point shackles, and unable to scratch yourself. This beautiful, brilliant, peaceful man has helped us to create a language and an understanding of where you can have the trauma… it was difficult for him to communicate… this can be happening in settings with compassionate medical personnel who are competent. I asked him: Who do you trust? What is your energetic? How do you feel? Despite the violent trauma, Mumia describes people who can be loving and caring.

There is care within prison settings and outside… there are competent, caring people who can operate in oppressive systems and do a good job. But there is a deep failure for the professional community. The medical community has to acknowledge the underlying oppressive violence that our community, our brothers, our sisters, our loved ones are suffering. The social determinants of health include… poverty, homelessness… violence. It is specifically state violence that is so important. When we look at medical assassination, there is medical complicity at the highest levels within these oppressive systems. Was that high blood sugar just missed? Quite possibly. Does that happen in outpatient settings? Absolutely. We're not saying that someone necessarily deliberately failed to diagnose. But… where there is objective evidence of an effort to assassinate, it is important that we all voice that state violence is so gross, so deliberate, that we need to be able to stand from a place of defense of our community.

CHAPTER EIGHT

How Prison Officials Manufactured Gangs and Gang Wars in Virginia's Prisons

Kevin "Rashid" Johnson

This 2024 article began as part of a larger article on abuses in Virginia's two remote supermax prisons, Red Onion and Wallens Ridge State Prisons. Readers felt the subject of the development of gangs and spread of gang wars in Virginia's prisons at the prompting of Virginia prison officials warranted an article of its own.

No Virginia Prison Gangs Before 2004

With the prevalence of youth lumpen organizations (so-called street gangs) in Virginia today, it's hard to believe that there were actually no gangs (especially no Black ones) in Virginia's prisons prior to 2004. The culture never took root because of Virginia's own culture of prisoners bonding based upon the cities they were from prevented it. The few gang members who did surface were mocked as bringing alien cultures into Virginia's own local culture. Virginia had always had a highly territorial culture against those from other states.

I witnessed the birth and clash of gangs in Virginia prisons and how officials at Virginia's remote Red Onion State Prison (ROSP) and Wallens Ridge (WRSP) manufactured the entire situation almost overnight beginning in 2005.

This all happened for a reason.

Inventing Justifications for Two Unneeded Supermaxes

The gangs were created and played against each other by these officials because they needed to create justifications for ROSP and WRSP to remain open in light of both being repeatedly exposed as unneeded, and previous justifications proving to be lies. Particularly where the expensive construction and operation of these prisons contributed to a state recession.

When ROSP and WRSP opened in 1998 and 1999 respectively, the Virginia Department of Corrections (*sic!*) (VDOC) director Ron Angelone fed the public the lie that these two 1,200-bed super-maximum security prisons were needed to safely house Virginia's huge number of chronically violent and dangerous prisoners and those never going home.

In response to a flood of prisoner complaints about racism and abuse at ROSP, Human Rights Watch (HRW) investigated conditions at the prison and in 1999 issued a scathing report.[1] The report not only exposed extreme racism and abuse in the prison, but also that Angelone's claimed justifications for these prisons were outright lies. HRW found that the vast majority of prisoners assigned to these facilities were soon to be released back to society while very few met the VDOC's own criteria for supermax housing, and the VDOC never had enough chronically disruptive prisoners to fill even a fraction of one let alone the two 1,200-bed supermax facilities. Officials then repeatedly rewrote VDOC classification policies attempting to make more prisoners qualify for housing at ROSP and WRSP, yet failed miserably.

They ended up having to transfer most ROSP and WRSP prisoners to lower-level facilities. Then began an unprecedented move of contracting to hold waves of prisoners from other states and territories. Large groups of prisoners were suddenly brought to ROSP and WRSP from Washington, DC, Connecticut, New Mexico, The Virgin Islands, Wyoming, and many other states in efforts to fill beds that the Virginia prisoners couldn't. This scheme quickly backfired as these out-of-state prisoners experienced the same racist abuse as had Virginia prisoners at the hands of ROSP and WRSP staff, and reported these mistreatments to loved ones, the media, and organizations in their home states, where they had strong advocacy networks and groups unlike Virginia prisoners.

Prisoners from Connecticut were being murdered by WRSP officials like Lawrence Frazier, a Black man who died from repeatedly being electrocuted by multiple guards while he was strapped down to a steel bedframe. There was the attempted murder (staged to look like a suicide) of another Connecticut prisoner, Michael Austin, a white man who WRSP guards disliked because he grew up around and embraced Black urban culture and clashed with WRSP rural white guards who ridiculed him and tried to influence him with racist values. Dozens of the New Mexico prisoners were systematically beaten upon intake at WRSP as were the Connecticut prisoners. The killing of Lawrence Frazier was also featured in the documentary *Up the Ridge* and an Amnesty International report on U.S. law enforcement officials' abuses of electric weapons.[2]

The pushback from advocates in their states was immediate! Large assemblies of families and groups from New

Mexico and Connecticut protested in the WRSP parking lot and nearby town of Big Stone Gap, VA. Pressure was brought to bear on officials in these prisoners' home states, several came to Virginia and toured WRSP. Lawsuits were filed and the media was awash with critical reports, especially about the abuses of the New Mexico and Connecticut prisoners at WRSP.

One by one these states terminated their contracts to house their prisoners at ROSP and WRSP, and Virginia was once again left with huge numbers of empty beds at these supermaxes. With no one to fill them and the need to give public justification for these prisons' continued expensive operations while facing waves of bad publicity, VDOC had once again to change the security classification of these prisons.

In 2005, WRSP had downgraded from supermax (security level 6) to maximum security (security level 5) prison, and for the first time WRSP became a predominantly general population (GP) prison. Meantime ROSP's population was cut in half from 1,200 to a little over 600 prisoners. A large number of minimum-security prisoners were then moved to ROSP ostensibly as custodial maintenance and other workers (called "cadre workers"); they were really just bed fillers.

But still other measures had to be taken to bring in more prisoners and fill more beds and justify these prisons. This is where the gang situation arises.

Creating Gangs to Justify These Prisons

At ROSP, the newly appointed warden, Tracey Ray, promoted a sergeant named Tony Adams who previously worked in the prison's dog kennel to the position of lead investigator and gang specialist (Adams was ROSP's first gang officer). Ray became warden in late 2004 and appointed Adams as investigator/gang specialist in early 2005. A low-ranking guard, James Bentley who still works as an investigator and gang specialist at ROSP today, was selected as Adams' assistant.

This new gang-busting duo hit the ground running alongside their WRSP counterpart Sgt. Steele. These men from rural white America with no prior exposure to Blacks or browns became self-proclaimed experts in urban Black and brown culture and street organizations overnight. Everywhere they went and looked they saw gang activity. And this wasn't accidental. They set out to *deliberately* create an organized gang problem and culture at these prisons where none existed before. This to validate their own jobs as "gang busters" and justify the continued operation of these prisons.

Before this period, the VDOC had no gang officials, no so-called STG (Security Threat Group) units nor task force, no policies on controlling gangs or gang activities, and so on, because there were no gangs in Virginia prisons.

At both ROSP and WRSP they created cellblocks in GP and solitary confinement exclusively for gang members unofficially called "gang pods." Those assigned to these pods were people they documented and labeled as gang members. In most cases, they targeted people who were, in fact, not in gangs. There had developed a small but insignificant gang presence at ROSP and WRSP under the influence of prisoners from other states like Connecticut and New York. But by placing prisoners who weren't gang members in blocks and cells with those who were, this led to waves of prisoners joining gangs for protection from those in these blocks who actually were gang members. It also created an isolated environment – like a hot house – where the gang culture took root and proliferated without resistance from Virginia's local culture. Most who weren't gang members when they entered these pods, were active gang members when they left. This created a steady cycle of non-members entering these pods and leaving as active members, so that the gang presence in these prisons multiplied overnight.

There were also some members of Central American gangs in the prisons (a result of large Salvadoran migrant communities in Alexandria, VA) who had traditional rivalries with certain Black gangs. Initially these browns stayed to themselves, but in the gang pods they clashed with those Blacks who had been profiled as members of the rival Black gangs. This also prompted Blacks who weren't initially in gangs to join them for protection or support-in-numbers against these brown gangs.

In violation of VDOC policy which required screening for gang affiliations and forbade housing documented gang rivals in cells together, Adams, Bentley, and their WRSP counterparts also deliberately put rivals in the same cells, especially Blacks and browns. Which predictably led to fights and stabbings, and cycles of revenge that they used as "proof" of organized gang violence. In fact, at WRSP administrators created a GP gang pod in a 44-cell cellblock, then moved documented rivals into the cells together. An hour later a large group of guards invaded the block and had all the prisoners stand outside their cells as they inspected their faces and hands for signs of fights. Those with marks on their faces or hands were written disciplinary infractions for being involved in "gang-related" fights – fights that officials themselves engineered. These and similar "documentations" were then used as "evidence" of a "problem with organized gang violence in Virginia prisons," for which WRSP and ROSP were now said to be needed to contain and control.

At ROSP and WRSP officials were manufacturing a gang presence and gang wars using a prison version of what Crips co-founder Stanley "Tookie" Williams observed "hood" cops and gang units did on the streets with the same outcome and purpose of justifying unneeded and abusive police and gang units. As Tookie described it in his book, *Blue Rage, Black Redemption:*

> Yes, America, as unbelievable as it may seem, had cops with impunity commit drivebys and other lawless acts. It was common practice for them to abduct a Crip or Bounty Hunter and drop him off in hostile territory, and then broadcast it over a loudspeaker. The predictable outcome was that the rival was either beaten or killed on the spot, which resulted in a cycle of payback. Cops would also inform opposing gangs where to find and attack a rival gang, and then say "Go handle your business."[3]

Like slaves, the gangs did exactly what their master commanded. Had they not been fueled by self-hatred, neither Crips, Bounty Hunters, nor any other Black gang would have been duped.

"The hood cops were pledged to protect and serve, but for us they were not there to help, but exploit us – and they were effective. With the cops' Machiavellian presence, the gang epidemic escalated. When gang warfare is fed and fueled by law enforcement, funds are generated for anti-gang units. Without gangs their units would no longer exist."

In an effort to isolate me since I'm not in any gangs and it was presumed that the gangs wouldn't interact with me, I was put in A-3, one of the solitary confinement gang pods at ROSP, where I witnessed the whole scheme play out. I watched the rivalries fester in that block, often under the direct instigation of guards who played sides with the gangs, then Adams, Bentley, and others would release rivals to the progressive housing gang pods where they were put in cells together and violence immediately erupted. Guards were openly amused by the stabbings and fights they were setting up.

When Gangs Become Conscious

I pointed out to those in the gang pod with me what was being done to them and how they were being used to justify the continued operations of ROSP and WRSP. Most agreed with what I pointed out and some refused to play into it. In 2010, I wrote an article, "Kill Yourself or Liberate Yourself," documenting the history of the U.S. government instigating and manipulating rivalries and wars between street gangs in just this manner and calling on them to unite and return to many of their original missions of serving our communities instead of preying on them. I also discussed the uses of the gang pods at ROSP in that article.[4]

My efforts began paying off as many of those in the cell-block with me embraced the views I shared with them and joined in the historic 2011 and 2013 hunger strikes led by thousands of California prisoners protesting solitary confinement. I was then transferred out of state in early 2012, followed the next year by several who participated in the 2013 strike.

One of the gang leaders, Kofi Dankur, aka L.I., who was a victim of the ROSP gang pods and out-of-state transfer where Virginia officials tried to set him and others up with racist white gangs in the other states (which they also did with me), wrote an article in 2022, "Blood in the Clenched Fist Alliance" (to which I wrote an introduction), where he bore witness to all of this. He opened the article stating:

> I've read Rashid's 2010 article "Kill Yourself or Liberate Yourself", and found it to contain perspectives which I also share. It also gives a true account of the scheme employed by Virginia officials at Red Onion State Prison to manufacture rival gang conflicts to create new justification for continuing to operate Virginia's two supermax prisons in remote southwestern Virginia – ROSP and WRSP, after both had been repeatedly discredited for racist abuse by their almost totally white staff against a predominantly Black prisoner population and exposed as unneeded. I was one of the numerous prisoners being housed at ROSP's so-called gang pods where these rivalries were manipulated by Virginia officials. I am an identified east coast Blood leader.[5]

While in the "gang pod" in 2010, I circulated a random survey to which 18 of the 22 prisoners in the cellblock immediately responded. The responses were telling, especially concerning the systemic false labeling of prisoners as gang members by "gang specialist" Sgt. Adams and others at ROSP and his role in putting rival gang members in cells together. I wrote an article discussing that survey and what it revealed about abuses at ROSP in the victims' own words.[6] Victims who mostly didn't communicate or get along with each other, spoke with one voice about conditions and mistreatments at ROSP.

As the gang wars became more deeply entrenched at ROSP and WRSP, many were transferred between other VDOC prisons across the state where the gang presence and conflicts followed and grew. From this process, I and others witnessed the literal creation of a huge gang presence and rivalries in Virginia's prisons where none previously existed, which also spread to the streets. All manufactured by officials at ROSP and WRSP, some of which still work at these prisons like James Bentley. The gang presence became so large and the resulting rival violence so extreme across Virginia's entire prison system that prisoners had to be separated and assigned to specific prison units based upon gang affiliations.

I was sent into domestic exile (transferred out of state) in early 2012 and returned to the Virginia prison system in late 2021. Upon my return, I found a different culture, whereas in most states, violent bangin' between rival gangs had largely stopped, while the local Virginia culture and gang culture have somewhat merged. Now there was still bonding based upon what city one is from but also a bonding across territories based upon gang affiliation. In many cases bonds based upon one's city of origin take priority over gang affiliation, while in other cases it's the reverse. The culture is still evolving.

If the public could have seen and known that prison officials caused the development and proliferation of gangs and gang wars in Virginia and the consequent violence and suffering endured by those in these prisons that spilled over into our outside communities, there would have definitely been massive push back against ROSP and WRSP. And there still should be push back now demanding that these places be closely scrutinized by the public and closed down. These remote prisons are a danger not benefit to their prisoners and the outside communities.

Dare To Struggle
Dare To Win! All Power To The
People!

CHAPTER NINE

The Pendleton 2 Defense Committee

their story

★ FREE THE PENDLETON 2 ★

On February 1, 1985, the Sons of Light, a KKK-splinter group of guards at the Indiana State Reformatory (now Pendleton Correctional Facility) sparked a prisoner rebellion with their brutal beating of defenseless prisoner Lincoln Love. According to a subsequent lawsuit, the white supremacist guards, armed with illegal billy clubs "maliciously held [Love] down and unmercifully stomped and kicked the inmate all over his body and hit the inmate upon and about his upper body and head with nightsticks." In a successful attempt to save his life, a politicized group of prisoners led by John "Balagoon" Cole and Christopher "Naeem" Trotter demanded entrance to the locked office where Lokmar was in chains & being beaten nearly to death. The Sons of Light turned & attacked them. As a result, the prisoners took hostages and occupied a cell block for 15 hours, demanding an end to censorship of letters, the ability to be politically active, minimum wages, and improvements to conditions so bad a court had deemed them "cruel and unusual punishment." John "Balagoon" Cole and Christopher "Naeem" Trotter were punished severely by the state for their sacrifice in saving a human life, receiving the sentences of 84 and 142 years respectively, with both held in solitary confinement for decades. Now they are both seniors facing major medical issues due to

DOC neglect. Yet, the white supremacist gang of guards that instigated it all, the Sons of Light, have been ignored for the last 39 years.

We, The Defense Committee to Free the Pendleton 2, demand:

1. The immediate release of John "Balagoon" Cole and Christopher "Naeem" Trotter from Indiana Department of Correction (IDOC) custody.
2. The immediate release of all incarcerated seniors and all medically vulnerable
3. The immediate release of all political prisoners.
4. A Federal investigation into the IDOC-condoned white supremacist guard gang, the Sons of Light.
5. A Federal investigation into formal and informal affiliations and activity of white supremacist guards in the IDOC.

Conclusion[1]

Joy James

War resistance is continuously waged against militarized police and (international) state violence that spread poverty, apartheid, and occupations. Forced to pay taxes that fund militarism and international arms deals, we counter genocides as we move beyond the normalization of Cop Cities in order to de-militarize predatory policing, prisons, and genocide. Through national and international struggles, we do more than survive. We thrive with defensive and offensive theories, strategies, and communities, and thus engage struggles with political education and revolutionary love.

Global encampments led by students, workers, communes have emerged to protest and to resist genocides in Palestine,[2] in Sudan,[3] against Rohingya in Myanmar,[4] and communities in West Papau.[5] The history of resistance against genocide is embedded in the 1951 document *We Charge Genocide*,[6] a document developed by the African American Civil Rights Congress (a unit of the Communist Party USA) and delivered to the United Nations by Paul Robeson. *We Charge Genocide* is notable for drawing international attention to crimes against African Americans, such as mob lynching and police brutality, economic and Labor exploitation, land and electoral theft, substandard schooling, housing, and medical care, imprisonment and predatory policing.

Raising the issue of genocide is inflammatory in the United States where administrations have inflicted global devastation.[7] Still, there are no ideological or moral justifications for the continuance of any state that finances the militarization of domestic policing and genocidal warfare against people under occupation. Communities and peoples have the right to resist apartheid and genocidal policies and structural terror and theft of their lands.

The U.S. is intimately familiar with genocidal violence given its origins as a nation. This might explain the nation's reluctance to grapple with its past, present, and future investment in genocides. (Neo)liberalism and (neo)conservatism dominate U.S. intellectual thought and deflect from genocidal violence against Indigenous and African peoples. Politicians, beholden to billionaires and Super Pacs,[8] largely ignore or abet anti-Black and anti-Indigenous, and anti-Muslim violence.

During his 2008 presidential electoral campaign, Democrat Barack Obama delivered a July 24 televised speech in Berlin, Germany that drew 200,000 multiracial people at an outdoor rally. The future U.S. president spoke of a "more perfect union" of global humanity. Condemning genocides, he challenged his audience: "Will we stand for the human rights of the dissident in Burma, the blogger in Iran, or the voter in Zimbabwe? Will we give meaning to the words 'never again' in Darfur?" Obama asserted: "The genocide of Darfur shames the conscience of us all." Apparently, it is easier for the U.S. to condemn a non-western, non-white nation for genocide than to charge western-style democracies for inflicting apartheid, occupations, and genocides.

Obama's address suggests that World War II was the "last good war" in which nations rallied to defeat the genocidal camps of Nazi Germany and end mass torture and murder of: Jews, Roma, "homosexuals," communists, Jehovah's Witnesses, Sinti, Slavic, Black and differently-abled people. Decades before the Nazi's dominated Europe,

Germany had inflicted genocide upon the Herero in Namibia.[9] Yet genocides continued despite the fact that the UN Convention on the Prevention and Punishment of Genocide prohibits:

> Intent to destroy, in whole or in part, a national, ethnical, racial or religious group, as such: (a) Killing members of the group; (b) Causing serious bodily or mental harm to members of the group; (c) Deliberately inflicting on the group conditions of life calculated to bring about its physical destruction in whole or in part; (d) Imposing measures intended to prevent births within the group; (e) Forcibly transferring children of the group to another group.[10]

According to João H. Costa Vargas, "genocide" should be recognized by the material conditions of loss, dishonor, violation, and violent death. The results of oppression—*not* the intent to oppress. Resistance to violence is key: "address, redress, and do away with what make possible the multiple facets of anti-Black genocide . . . dehumanizing values . . . reproduced by the systematic and persistent disregard for the lives of Afro-descended individuals and their communities."[11] If the focus is upon *intent* to harm, not actual harm, the burden of proof is placed on the victims or targets and legalistic not ethical discourse dominates.[12] International and U.S. law mandate that genocidal states be disciplined and their capacity to inflict harm neutralized. Moving beyond Cop Cities, we build what the state refuses: caretaking and protesting that shift into movements that build marronage and resist militarized policing and warfare. Thus, we shift through stages to build, defend and stabilize sanctuaries and protections to quell Cop Cities, apartheid, and genocide.

We Remember the Attempts to be Free: Part 3

By James Jones (inspired by Joy James)

it was an inspiring display of love, resistance, and rebellion when the Palestinian people began to claw, climb, and break the gates that surrounded them in the 2018 March of Return. Their hearts cried for liberation; revolutionary love was in the air. These beautiful sounds of resistance were shattered by gunfire from armed troops ordered to guard the gates and prevent anyone from exiting the murderous enclosure that had long trapped masses through intimidation, hatred, and the threat of death.

It is the love of the people that moves them to rattle the gates even in the face of death. This is an incisive answer to the poignant question posed by Joy James, "where is revolutionary love?" As James observes, the answer depends in part on where you are standing and with whom. The beauty of humanity is the endurance and transcendence of our spirit, the ability to stand together as a people even when we are worlds apart.

Resistance can be spontaneous or organized but it is always galvanized by love. So rattle the fences of Gaza or run for the gates of Soledad. George Jackson's murder was also "justified" by claims that he ran for the prison gates. He was killed by prison guards, whose barrage of bullets tore through his body. His life and murder inspired the uprising inside the walls of Attica one month later.

The people of Palestine and the people in prison – these are the unified masses held captive, surrounded and obstructed by gates erected to keep them from traveling freely and actualizing their dreams. In the words of Joy James, "You have the right if people are torturing you, if you are being raped if you're being starved or beaten. If you've been thrown in the hole so that you can have a nervous breakdown or become psychotic · you get to run. If you have a torturer you get to try to leave the enclosure. But heed the gruesome caveat, they will shoot you for it."

And from what we see in the media today, the state will spread misinformation and propaganda to justify its violent and oppressive measures, whether you're enclosed inside a prison or a geographical border constructed to contain the world's surplus populations and those designated for ethnic cleansing. But even under the threat of imminent death, we still rattle the cage.

We stand in solidarity with Palestine, we remember Attica, and we honor the legacies of George and Jonathan Jackson. In the words of Joy James, "We remember the attempts to be free."

Text by James Jones, art illustration by Mon M.

QR Code/Omeka Site

Notes

Introduction

1. See R. J. Rico, "'Stop Cop City' Petition Campaign in Limbo as Atlanta Officials Refuse to Process Signatures." AP, NPR, September 11, 2023; www.pbs.org/newshour/politics/stop-cop-city-petition-campaign-in-limbo-as-atlanta-officials-refuse-to-process-signatures. Also see: Prem Thakker, "Atlanta Mayor Dismisses Cop City Referendum as 'Not an Election'." *The Intercept*, September 27, 2023.

2. Kamau Franklin, the founder of Community Movement Builders (CMB), has become the public spokesperson on Atlanta's Cop City. Popular press offer recent critiques of funding to Stop Cop City as a "movement." It is not fully discussed in public the impact of millions of dollars from (non)corporate donors/millionaires has on grassroots organizations' capacity to radically resist poverty and police brutality with autonomous and creative responses not directed or influenced by donors. (One notes that nonprofits are *not* generally considered to be *grassroots* organizations directed by the working class and most vulnerable, impacted sectors.) Franklin's X account, however, points to an alternative perspective in a link (accessed April 25, 2024) to *Scenes from the Atlanta Forest*, https://scenes.noblogs.org/. This publication is authored by nonpacifist (and likely nonduopoly voter) activists who detail their analyses and condemnations of universities, aligned with corporate donors, that are complicit in predatory warfare against environmentalists and nonelite communities.

   For diverse perspectives on funding streams independent of decision-making by the working class and impoverished, see: "As Corporations Step Back, It's Our Time to Step Up." Philanthropy News Digest, *Forbes*, February 27, 2024; Julia

Wallace et al., "Bring BLM Back to the Streets: A Critique of the M4BL Platform." *Left Voice*, December 30, 2016; and Joy James, *New Bones Abolition*. Philadelphia, PA: Common Notions, 2023.

3. Prem Thakker. "Atlanta Officials Unveil Onerous Verification Requirements for Cop City Referendum." *The Intercept*, August 21, 2023. https://theintercept.com/2023/08/21/atlanta-cop-city-referendum-signatures/.

4. Jessenia Class. "Corporations are Keeping Cop City Alive." *The Flaw*, May 13, 2023. https://theflaw.org/articles/corporations-are-keeping-cop-city-alive/#:~:text=Backed%20in%20turn%20by%20a,the%20media%20narrative%20around%20protest.

5. Sam Levin, "'It Never Stops': Killings by US Police Reach Record High in 2022." *The Guardian*, January 6, 2023.

6. See David Peisner, "Fergie Chambers Is Heir to One of America's Richest Families – and Determined to See the U.S. Fall." *The Rolling Stone*, March 24, 2024. www.rollingstone.com/culture/culture-features/fergie-chambers-cox-enterprises-heir-overthrow-us-1234983156/.

    See Kiera Butler, "There Is a Communist Multimillionaire Fomenting Revolution in Atlanta." *Mother Jones*, March 21, 2024. www.motherjones.com/politics/2024/03/theres-a-communist-multi-millionaire-fomenting-revolution-in-atlanta/.

7. For an analytic of Captive Maternal stages in struggle, see J. James, *In Pursuit of Revolutionary Love*. London: Divided, 2023; *New Bones Abolition*. Philadelphia, PA: Common Notions, 2023; "The Womb of Western Theory," *Carceral Notebooks*, 2014. https://sites.williams.edu/jjames/files/2019/05/WombofWesternTheory2016.pdf.

Chapter One

1. "The Rubik's Cube of Cop City" was first published in *Inquest*, July 18, 2023.

2. Kaitlyn Radde, "Autopsy Reveals Anti-'Cop City' Activist's Hands Were Raised When Shot and Killed." *NPR*,

March 11, 2023. www.npr.org/2023/03/11/1162843992/
cop-city-atlanta-activist-autopsy.

Nick Valencia, Devon M. Sayers, and Pamela Kirkland.
"Climate Activist Killed in 'Cop City' Protest Sustained 57
Gunshot Wounds, Official Autopsy Says, but Questions
about Gunpowder Residue Remain." *CNN*, April 20, 2023.
www.cnn.com/2023/04/20/us/cop-city-activist-killed-
dekalb-county-medical-examiner/index.html.

3. Kaitlyn Radde, "Autopsy Reveals Anti-'Cop City' Activist's
Hands Were Raised When Shot and Killed."

Valencia, Sayers, and Kirkland. "Climate Activist Killed in
'Cop City' Protest Sustained 57 Gunshot Wounds."

4. R.J. Rico, "Muddy Clothes? 'Cop City' Activists Question
Police Evidence." *AP News*, March 24, 2023. https://apnews.
com/article/cop-city-protest-domestic-terrorism-atlanta-6d1
14e109d489d316f588f51c7cabocc.

5. *The Associated Press.* "3 Atlanta Activists are Arrested After
Their Fund Bailed Out Protesters of 'Cop City.'" *NPR*, June
1, 2023. www.npr.org/2023/06/01/1179427542/atlanta-
copy-city-arrests.

6. Kate Brumback, "Bond Granted for 3 Activists Whose Fund
Bailed Out People Protesting Atlanta 'Cop City' Project."
AP News, June 2, 2023. https://apnews.com/article/police-
training-center-arrests-cop-city-1468a138ed4b17ed394e4b
1e4fe202fe.

7. Matt Scott. "APD, Gbi Raid Bail Fund, Arrest Three Organizers." Atlanta Community Press Collective, June 12, 2023.
https://atlpresscollective.com/2023/05/31/apd-gbi-raid-
bail-fund-arrest-three-organizers/.

8. "Statement from the Atlanta Solidarity Fund Regarding
Attorney General's Investigation into Transactions, Donors."
Document Cloud, June 2, 2023. Atlanta Solidarity Fund.
www.documentcloud.org/documents/23833003-atlanta-
solidarity-fund-investigation-response-statement-1-docx-1.

9. Jon Ossof. Twitter post, June 4, 2023. https://twitter.com/
ossoff/status/1665436838956347392.

10. Taiyler S. Mitchell, "Dem Lawmakers Speak Out Against
Cop City Arrests." *HuffPost*, June 5, 2023. www.huffpost.

com/entry/lawmakers-cop-city-arrests-atlanta_n_647cf7a3e
4b02325c5e1608e.

11. R.J. Rico, "'Stop Cop City' Activists Pack Atlanta City Hall
Ahead of Crucial Vote." *AP News*, June 6, 2023. https://
apnews.com/article/cop-city-vote-atlanta-city-council-
d782604c15874e441570654ea362e0ef.

12. Dyana Bagby and Collin Kelley, "Live Coverage: Atlanta
City Council Approves 'Cop City' Funding after Hundreds
Speak for 15 Hours." *Georgia Public Broadcasting*, June 6,
2023. www.gpb.org/news/2023/06/06/live-coverage-atlanta-
city-council-approves-cop-city-funding-after-hundreds-
speak.

13. R.J. Rico, "Atlanta Clerk Sued for Denying 'Stop Cop City'
Petition Lets Effort Move Forward." *ABC News*, June 21,
2023. https://abcnews.go.com/US/wireStory/atlanta-clerk-
sued-denying-stop-cop-city-petition-100287575.

14. *Associated Press*, "Atlanta Police Training Center Opponents
Sue over Delays in Approving Referendum." *NBCNews.
com*, June 20, 2023. www.nbcnews.com/news/nbcblk/atlanta-
police-training-center-opponents-sue-delays-approving-
referend-rcna90252.

15. R.J. Rico, "Atlanta Organizers Unveil Plan to Take 'Cop City'
Fight to the Ballot Box." *PBS*, June 7, 2023. www.pbs.org/
newshour/politics/atlanta-organizers-unveil-plan-to-take-
cop-city-fight-to-the-ballot-box. Gloria Tatum, "Forest
Defenders Reoccupy Weelaunee to Stop Cop City." *People's
Tribune*, March 12, 2023. https://peoplestribune.org/2023/03/
forest-defenders-reoccupy-weelaunee-to-stop-cop-city/.

16. Gloria Tatum, "Native Americans Share Concerns over
Fate of Forest." *Streets of Atlanta*, May 3, 2022. https://
streetsofatlanta.blog/2022/05/02/native-americans-share-
concerns-over-fate-of-forest/; "Native Knowledge 360°: The
Removal of the Muscogee Nation." National Museum of the
American Indian. Accessed 2023.

17. "21st Century Community Policing." Atlanta Police
Foundation. Accessed 2023. https://atlantapolicefoundation.
org/.

18. Sam Levin, "'It Never Stops': Killings by US Police Reach Record High in 2022." *The Guardian*, January 6, 2023. www.theguardian.com/us-news/2023/jan/06/us-police-killings-record-number-2022.

19. Addie Haney, "Atlanta Police Down 220 Officers since Start of January, Department Says." *11Alive.com*, December 9, 2020. www.11alive.com/article/news/local/atlanta-police-numbers-2020/85-a54ace87-bed2-4d41-87b1-150a9b87 7672.

20. "21st Century Community Policing." Atlanta Police Foundation. Accessed 2023. https://atlantapolicefoundation.org/.

21. Ibid.

22. Youth Justice Project. "Projection: Spoken Word Performance by Hausson Byrd." YouTube video, 3:28. www.youtube.com/watch?v=XLptzN_zvBo.

Chapter Two

1. Youth Justice Project. "Projection: Spoken Word Performance by Hausson Byrd." YouTube video, 3:28. www.youtube.com/watch?v=XLptzN_zvBo. Rev. Matthew V. Johnson and Joy James. "A Letter of Concern to Black Clergy Regarding 'Cop City.'" *Logos Journal*, June 14, 2023. https://logosjournal.com/2023/a-letter-of-concern-to-black-clergy-regarding-cop-city/.

2. "Introducing the Economic Future for African People." The African People's Socialist Party. Accessed 2023. https://apspuhuru.org/about/black-star-industries/. Azadeh Shahshahani and Collin P. Poirot. "The DOJ Is Using 'Foreign Agents' Accusations to Repress Black Liberation Organizers." *The Nation*, April 26, 2023. www.thenation.com/article/politics/foreign-agents-registration-act-political-repression/.

3. Ursula Wolfe-Rocca. "Why We Should Teach About the FBI's War on the Civil Rights Movement." *Zinn Education Project*, March 1, 2016. www.zinnedproject.org/if-we-knew-our-history/fbi-war-civil-rights-movement/.

4. Nina D. Howland, David C. Humphrey, and Harriet D. Schwar, eds. *Foreign Relations of the United States*, 1964–1968, Volume XXIII, Document 1, Congo, 1960–1968. Washington, DC: Government Printing Office, 2013. https://history.state.gov/historicaldocuments/frus1964-68v23.

5. David Dennis, "How Dick Gregory Forced the FBI to Find the Bodies of Three Civil Rights Workers Slain in Mississippi." *Medium*, August 30, 2017. https://stillcrew.com/how-dick-gregory-forced-the-fbi-to-find-the-bodies-of-goodman-chaney-and-schwerner-fa9790c49ad4.

6. Michael Beschloss, "'Think They Got Killed?' 1964, L.B.J. and Three Civil Rights Icons." *The New York Times*, June 25, 2014. www.nytimes.com/2014/06/26/upshot/think-they-got-killed-1964-lbj-and-three-civil-rights-icons.html.

7. "June 21, 1964: Three Civil Rights Workers Murdered in Mississippi." *Zinn Education Project*, June 21, 2021. www.zinnedproject.org/news/tdih/chaney-goodman-schwerner-murdered/.

8. "16 Senior Police and Public Safety Executives Return from Police Executive Training in Israel." *Georgia State News Hub*, November 19, 2021. Andrew Young School of Policy Studies. https://news.gsu.edu/2021/11/19/16-senior-police-and-public-safety-executives-return-from-police-executive-training-in-israel/.

9. Ariella Roitman. "Georgia State Police Return Home after Two-Week Israeli Training." *The Jerusalem Post* JPost.com, July 22, 2022. www.jpost.com/israeli-news/article-711682.

10. Council on American-Islamic Relations. "BIGOTRY & BRUTALITY IN FOREIGN POLICE TRAINING: A Comprehensive Report on the Georgia International Law Enforcement Exchange (GILEE)." Council on American-Islamic Relations, 2020. www.jstor.org/stable/resrep31111.

11. UNHRC, Report of the independent international commission of inquiry on the protests in the Occupied Palestinian Territory, 25 February–22 March 2019. www.ohchr.org/sites/default/files/Documents/HRBodies/HRCouncil/CoIOPT/A_HRC_40_74.pdf.

Nick Cumming-Bruce. "Israelis May Have Committed Crimes Against Humanity in Gaza Protests, U.N. Says." *The New York Times*, February 28, 2019. www.nytimes.com/2019/02/28/world/middleeast/israel-crimes-against-humanity-gaza-un.html.

12. "Israel's Occupation: 50 Years of Dispossession." Amnesty International. Accessed 2023. www.amnesty.org/en/latest/campaigns/2017/06/israel-occupation-50-years-of-dispossession/#:~:text=Since%20the%20occupation%20first%20began,them%20of%20their%20basic%20rights. Valentina Azarova. "Towards a Counter-Hegemonic Law of Occupation: The Regulation of Predatory Interstate Acts in Contemporary International Law." *Yearbook of International Humanitarian Law*, January 1, 2018. https://ssrn.com/abstract=3133978.

13. Jessenia Class. "Corporations Are Keeping Cop City Alive." *The Flaw*, May 13, 2023. https://theflaw.org/articles/corporations-are-keeping-cop-city-alive/#:~:text=Backed%20in%20turn%20by%20a,the%20media%20narrative%20around%20protest.

Derek Seidman. "Corporate Backers of the Blue: How Corporations Bankroll U.S. Police Foundations." *Eyes on the Ties*, June 18, 2020. https://news.littlesis.org/2020/06/18/corporate-backers-of-the-blue-how-corporations-bankroll-u-s-police-foundations/.

14. Selam Gebrekidan, Matt Apuzzo, Catherine Porter, and Constant Méheut. "Invade Haiti, Wall Street Urged. The U.S. Obliged." *The New York Times*, May 20, 2022. www.nytimes.com/2022/05/20/world/haiti-wall-street-us-banks.html. The United Fruit Company and the 1954 Guatemalan Coup, 2023. https://ufcguatemala.voices.wooster.edu/. Benjamin Harrison. "The United States and the 1909 Nicaragua Revolution." *Caribbean Quarterly* 41, no. 3/4 (1995): 45–63.www.jstor.org/stable/40653942. Becky Little. "10 Times America Helped Overthrow a Foreign Government." *History.com*, June 7, 2022. www.history.com/news/us-overthrow-foreign-governments.

15. Square Mile Media Atlanta. "55 TRINITY – 'I DON'T WANT COP CITY' Rev. Keyanna Jones." Youtube, 6:06. March 6, 2023. www.youtube.com/watch?v=tnFbsm3k2Oc.

16. Rev. Keyanna Jones. "Atlanta's Black Community Says, 'Stop Cop City!'" Interview with Margaret Kimberley. *Black Agenda Report*. Podcast audio. June 9, 2023. www.blackagendareport.com/atlantas-black-community-says-stop-cop-city.

17. "Cop City Archives." *Scalawag*, 2023. https://scalawagmagazine.org/tag/cop-city/. Department of the Navy. Military Operations on Urbanized Terrain (MOUT).

18. Department of the Army. URBAN TERRAIN ANALYSIS TRAINING AIDS. Washington, DC: Department of the Army, 1981. https://apps.dtic.mil/sti/tr/pdf/ADA105652.pdf.

19. Lesley Gill, *The School of the Americas: Military Training and Political Violence in the Americas*. Durham, NC: Duke University Press, September 2004. www.dukepress.edu/the-school-of-the-americas.

20. Julia Wright. "France's Racism Still on Display as It Denies Its Colonial Past – and Present," *Truthout*, July 12, 2023. https://truthout.org/articles/frances-racism-still-on-display-as-it-denies-its-colonial-past-and-present/?utm_source=Truthout&utm_campaign=36ae1adeod-EMAIL_CAMPAIGN_3_20_2023_13_41_COPY_05&utm_medium=email&utm_term=0_bbb541a1db-36ae1adeod-650623509&mc_cid=36ae1adeod&mc_eid=62fe682022.

21. Amilcar Cabral, *Return to the Source: Selected Speeches*. Edited by Africa Information Service. NYU Press, 1973. https://abahlali.org/wp-content/uploads/2016/12/amilcar_cabral_return_to_the_source-ilovepdf-compressed.pdf.

Chapter Three

1. This chapter is an excerpt from *Logos: Journal of Modern Society and Culture*, 2024, Vol 3, No. 1, https://logosjournal.com/article/a-letter-of-concern-to-black-clergy-regarding-cop-city/.

Chapter Five

1. See Chamian Cruz, "Personnel Files Released of State Troopers Who Fatally Shot 'Cop City' Activist One Year Ago." *WABE*, January 18, 2024. www.wabe.org/personnel-files-released-of-state-troopers-who-fatally-shot-cop-city-activist-one-year-ago/.

Chapter Six

1. For information on Black self-defense for half a millennial, see: Jordan Engel, "500 Years of Black Resistance," Decolonial Atlas, 2018, https://decolonialatlas.wordpress.com/wp-content/uploads/2018/02/500-years-of-black-resistance.jpg.
2. See "Stop Cop City," Community Movement Builders. https://communitymovementbuilders.org/stop-cop-city/; Renee Johnson, "Cop Cities USA." Is Your Life Better. https://isyourlifebetter.net/cop-cities-usa/.

Chapter Seven

1. This abbreviated interview was first published in *San Francisco Bay*, February 27, 2024. https://sfbayview.com/2024/02/assassination-attempts-against-mumia-abu-jamal/. The transcript is taken from a February BPM/RSTV interview with Kalonji Changa and Joy James: www.youtube.com/watch?v=9qUTtQiopPo.
2. See Mumia Abu-Jamal and Jennifer Black, *Beneath the Mountain: An Anti-Prison Reader*. San Francisco, CA: City Lights, 2024. https://citylights.com/city-lights-published/beneath-the-mountain-an-anti-prison-re/.
3. See *State Crime Journal*, Pluto Journal, Volume 12, Issue 2, March 6, 2024, with articles on Mumia Abu-Jamal and Palestine. www.scienceopen.com/journal-issue?id=bf18813f-d2f3-43c7-bf36-79709744b1e8.

Chapter Eight

1. Jamie Fellner, "Red Onion State Prison: Super-Maximum Security Confinement in Virginia." Human Rights Watch, 1999. www.hrw.org/reports/1999/redonion.
2. Amnesty International, "Cruelty in Control? The Stun Belt and Other Electroshock Weapons in Law Enforcement," 2002. http://totse2.com/totse/end/law/justice_for_all/6resforu.htm.
3. Stanley "Tookie" Williams, *Blue Rage, Black Redemption*.
4. Kevin "Rashid" Johnson, "Kill Yourself or Liberate Yourself: The Real U.S. Imperialist Policy on Gang Violence Versus the Revolutionary Alternative," 2010. http://rashidmod.com/?p=6264.
5. Kofi Donkur, a.k.a. L.I., "Blood in the Clenched Fist Alliance," 2022. http://rashidmod.com/?p=3195.
6. Kevin "Rashid" Johnson, "When Given a Voice the Voiceless Speak as One: A Random Survey Confirms Racism, Abuse, and Corruption at Virginia's Red Onion State Prison," 2010. http://rashidmod.com/?p=435.

Conclusion

1. This Conclusion revisits and adapts a previously published article: Joy James, "The Dead Zone: Stumbling at the Crossroads of Party Politics, Genocide, and Post-Racial Racism," *South Atlantic Quarterly* 108:3, Summer 2009, Duke University Press.
2. "South Africa levels accusations of 'genocidal conduct' against Israel at UN Int'l Court of Justice," United Nations. www.youtube.com/watch?v=oQ_zTb9dfGU.
3. Human Rights Watch, "Sudan: New Mass Ethnic Killings, Pillage in Darfur," November 26, 2023. www.hrw.org/news/2023/11/26/sudan-new-mass-ethnic-killings-pillage-darfur.

4. "European Nations Join Myanmar Genocide Case," Al Jazeera, November 17, 2023.

5. Darius Shahtahmasebi, "West Papau: The Genocide That is Being Ignored by the World," *Indigenous Peoples Major Group for Sustainable Development*, nd. www.indigenouspeoples-sdg.org/index.php/english/ttt/1081-west-papua-the-genocide-that-is-being-ignored-by-the-world.

6. Susan A. Glenn, "We Charge Genocide – The 1951 Black Lives Matter Campaign," Mapping American Social Movements Project, University of Washington. https://depts.washington.edu/moves/CRC_genocide.shtml

7. Despite the official lies—told by President George W. Bush, Dick Cheney, Condoleezza Rice, Colin Powell, et al. about Iraqi weapons of mass destruction, no one was impeached or forced to resign from office due to a twenty-years+ war that destabilized the Middle East and led to the destruction of Iraq's infrastructure, the death and maiming of nearly one million people, and the displacement of millions more as internal and external refugees.

8. Open Secrets, Super Pacs. www.opensecrets.org/political-action-committees-pacs/super-pacs/2022.

9. "Herero & Nama Disagree on Germany-Namibia Genocide-Compensation Deal," DW News. www.youtube.com/watch?v=70ECgCzNtxQ.

10. www.un.org/en/genocideprevention/documents/publications-and-resources/Genocide_Convention_75th Anniversary_2023.pdf.

11. João H. Costa Vargas, *Never Meant to Survive: Genocide and Utopias in Black Diaspora Communities*, Rowman & Littlefield, 2008.

12. President Ronald Reagan signed and enacted the UN genocide treaty in 1988, after the U.S. Senate amended it (allegedly in order to restrict its usage by Native Americans and African Americans). The *NYT* quotes Reagan:

    Mr. Reagan said he would have preferred a bill that established the death penalty for genocidal crimes but said, "This legislation still represents a strong and clear statement by the United States that it will punish acts of genocide with the force of law and the righteousness of justice."

See Steven V. Roberts, "Reagan Signs Bill Ratifying U.N. Genocide Pact," *New York Times*, November 5, 1988.

"We Remember the Attempts to Be Free"

James Jones's "We Remember the Attempts to Be Free, Part 3," with illustration by Mon M, circulated as a poster-text image in November 2023. The poster references Joy James's August 12, 2021, interview with *Millennials Are Killing Capitalism*. That interview was transcribed and edited into the final two chapters in James's podcast-based book *In Pursuit of Revolutionary Love* (London: Divided, 2022). Contributing an original "Part 3" to the book, linking the abolition of (political) prisoners and Palestinians, Jones calls for freedoms beyond prisons and occupations.

Bibliography

Al Jazeera Staff, "Atlanta's 'Cop City' and the debate over US protest rights," Al Jazeera, March 8, 2023. www.aljazeera.com/news/2023/3/8/atlantas-cop-city-and-the-debate-over-us-protests.

Abu-Jamal, Mumia, and Jennifer Black, *Beneath the Mountain: An Anti-Prison Reader.* San Francisco, CA: City Lights, 2024. https://citylights.com/city-lights-published/beneath-the-mountain-an-anti-prison-re/.

Anonymous, "The Story of FTP IV: Bronx Bloody Thursday." June 4, 2020.

Anonymous, "The City in the Forest." Crimethinc.com, April 11, 2022.

Anonymous, "Living in an Earthquake: The Fight Against Cop City Confronts Unprecedented Repression." Crimethinc.com, 2023.

Anonymous, "The Forest in the City: Two Years of Forest Defense in Atlanta." Crimethinc.com, February 22, 2023.

Associated Press. "Atlanta Police Training Center Opponents Sue over Delays in Approving Referendum." *NBCNews.com*, June 20, 2023. www.nbcnews.com/news/nbcblk/atlanta-police-training-center-opponents-sue-delays-approving-referend-rcna90252.

Associated Press. "3 Atlanta Activists Are Arrested After Their Fund Bailed Out Protesters of 'Cop City.'" NPR, June 1, 2023. www.npr.org/2023/06/01/1179427542/atlanta-copy-city-arrests.

Atlanta Community Press Collective, "Tell Liliana Bakhtiari and Jason Dozier it's time to Stop Cop City!" https://atlpresscollective.com/2022/09/30/tell-liliana-bakhtiari-and-jason-dozier-its-time-to-stop-cop-city/.

"The Atlanta Police Foundation." Atlanta Police Foundation. Accessed 2023. https://atlantapolicefoundation.org/about-the-atlanta-police-foundation/.

Azarova, Valentina. "Towards a Counter-Hegemonic Law of Occupation: The Regulation of Predatory Interstate Acts in Contemporary International Law." *Yearbook of International Humanitarian Law*, January 1, 2018. https://ssrn.com/abstract=3133978.

Bagby, Dyana, and Collin Kelley. "Live Coverage: Atlanta City Council Approves 'Cop City' Funding after Hundreds Speak for 15 Hours." *Georgia Public Broadcasting*, June 6, 2023. www.gpb.org/news/2023/06/06/live-coverage-atlanta-city-council-approves-cop-city-funding-after-hundreds-speak.

Beschloss, Michael. "'Think They Got Killed?' 1964, L.B.J. and Three Civil Rights Icons." *The New York Times*, June 25, 2014. www.nytimes.com/2014/06/26/upshot/think-they-got-killed-1964-lbj-and-three-civil-rights-icons.html.

Black Power Media. "Resisting Cop City Corporate and Clergy Colonizers." Youtube, 1:17:28. July 18, 2023, www.youtube.com/watch?v=31Fe4g5Iu54.

Brumback, Kate. "Bond Granted for 3 Activists Whose Fund Bailed Out People Protesting Atlanta 'Cop City' Project." *AP News*, June 2, 2023.

Butler, Kiera, "There's a Communist Multimillionaire Fomenting Revolution in Atlanta." *Mother Jones*, March 21, 2024.

Cabral, Amilcar. "Return to the Source: Selected Speeches, 1974". https://abahlali.org/wp-content/uploads/2016/12/amilcar_cabral_return_to_the_source-ilovepdf-compressed.pdf.

Class, Jessenia. "Corporations are Keeping Cop City Alive." *The Flaw*, May 13, 2023. https://theflaw.org/articles/corporations-are-keeping-cop-city-alive/#:~:text=Backed%20in%20turn%20by%20a,the%20media%20narrative%20around%20protest.

"Cop City Archives." *Scalawag*, 2023. https://scalawagmagazine.org/tag/cop-city/. Department of the Navy. Military Operations on Urbanized Terrain (MOUT).

Costa Vargas. João H., *Never Meant to Survive: Genocide and Utopias in Black Diaspora Communities*, Rowman & Littlefield, 2008.

Council on American-Islamic Relations. "BIGOTRY & BRUTALITY IN FOREIGN POLICE TRAINING: A Comprehensive Report on the Georgia International Law Enforcement Exchange (GILEE)." Council on American-Islamic Relations, 2020. www.jstor.org/stable/resrep31111.

Cruz, Chamian. "Personnel Files Released of State Troopers Who Fatally Shot 'Cop City' Activist One Year Ago." *WABE*, January 18, 2024. www.wabe.org/personnel-files-released-of-state-troopers-who-fatally-shot-cop-city-activist-one-year-ago/.

Cumming-Bruce, Nick. "Israelis May Have Committed Crimes Against Humanity in Gaza Protests, U.N. Says." *The New York Times*, February 28, 2019. www.nytimes.com/2019/02/28/world/middleeast/israel-crimes-against-humanity-gaza-un.html.

Dennis, David. "How Dick Gregory Forced the FBI to Find the Bodies of Three Civil Rights Workers Slain in Mississippi." *Medium*, August 30, 2017. https://stillcrew.com/how-dick-gregory-forced-the-fbi-to-find-the-bodies-of-goodman-chaney-and-schwerner-fa9790c49ad4.

Department of the Army. *Urban Terrain Analysis Training Aids*. Washington, DC: Department of the Army, 1981. https://apps.dtic.mil/sti/tr/pdf/ADA105652.pdf.

Enriquez, Alyza. "Atlanta Police Release Body Camera Footage of Activist Killing at 'Cop City.'" *VICE*, February 9, 2023. www.vice.com/en/article/wxnvgx/atlanta-police-release-body-camera-footage-of-activist-killing-at-cop-city.

Gebrekidan, Selam, Matt Apuzzo, Catherine Porter, and Constant Méheut. "Invade Haiti, Wall Street Urged. The U.S. Obliged." *The New York Times*, May 20, 2022.

Gill, Lesley, *The School of the Americas: Military Training and Political Violence in the Americas*. Durham, NC: Duke University Press, September 2004. www.dukeupress.edu/the-school-of-the-americas.

Glenn, Susan A., "We Charge Genocide – The 1951 Black Lives Matter Campaign." Mapping American Social Movements Project, University of Washington.

Guardian, "'I'm so scared, please come': Hind Rajab, six, found dead in Gaza 12 days after cry for help," Guardian, February 10, 2024. www.theguardian.com/world/2024/feb/10/im-so-scared-please-come-hind-rajab-six-found-dead-in-gaza-12-days-after-cry-for-help.

Haney, Addie. "Atlanta Police Down 220 Officers since Start of January, Department Says." *11Alive.com*, December 9, 2020. www.11alive.com/article/news/local/atlanta-police-numbers-2020/85-a54ace87-bed2-4d41-87b1-150a9b877672.

Harrison, Benjamin. "The United States and the 1909 Nicaragua Revolution." *Caribbean Quarterly* 41, no. 3/4 (1995): 45–63. www.jstor.org/stable/40653942.

Hirshkind, Micah, "The fight to Stop Cop City has decades-old roots." PRISM, March 2, 2023.

Howland, Nina D., David C. Humphrey, and Harriet D. Schwar, eds. *Foreign Relations of the United States, 1964–1968*, Volume XXIII, Document 1, Congo, 1960–1968. Washington, DC: Government Printing Office, 2013. https://history.state.gov/historicaldocuments/frus1964-68v23.

Human Rights Watch, "Sudan: New Mass Ethnic Killings, Pillage in Darfur." November 26, 2023.

"Introducing the Economic Future for African People." The African People's Socialist Party. Accessed 2023.

"Israel's Occupation: 50 Years of Dispossession." Amnesty International. Accessed 2023. www.amnesty.org/en/latest/campaigns/2017/06/israel-occupation-50-years-of-dispossession/#:~:text=Since%20the%20occupation%20first%20began,them%20of.

James, Joy, "The Dead Zone: Stumbling at the Crossroads of Party Politics, Genocide, and Post-Racial Racism." *South Atlantic Quarterly* 108:3, Summer 2009, Duke University Press.

Johnson, Rashid "Kevin", "Kill Yourself or Liberate Yourself: The Real U.S. Imperialist Policy on Gang Violence vs. The Revolutionary Alternative," June 19, 2011.

Johnson, Renee. "Cop Cities USA," Is Your Life Better. Accessed 2024. https://isyourlifebetter.net/cop-cities-usa/.

Johnson, Rev. Matthew V., and Joy James. "A Letter of Concern to Black Clergy Regarding 'Cop City.'" *Logos Journal*, June 14, 2023. https://logosjournal.com/2023/a-letter-of-concern-to-black-clergy-regarding-cop-city/.

Jones, James, Mon M (illustrator). "We Remember the Attempts to be Free," Part 3. November 2023 circulation; reference from *In Pursuit of Revolutionary Love.*

Jones, Rev. Keyanna (Atlanta's Black Community Says, "Stop Cop City!"). Interview with Margaret Kimberley. *Black Agenda Report*. Podcast audio. June 9, 2023. www.blackagendareport.com/atlantas-black-community-says-stop-cop-city.

"June 21, 1964: Three Civil Rights Workers Murdered in Mississippi." Zinn Education Project, June 21, 2021. www.zinnedproject.org/news/tdih/chaney-goodman-schwerner-murdered/.

Lennard, Natasha, and Akela Lacy. "Activists Face Felonies for Distributing Flyers on 'Cop City' Protester Killing." *The Intercept*, May 2, 2023.

Levin, Sam. "'It Never Stops': Killings by US Police Reach Record High in 2022." *The Guardian*, January 6, 2023. www.theguardian.com/us-news/2023/jan/06/us-police-killings-record-number-2022.

Little, Becky. "10 Times America Helped Overthrow a Foreign Government." *History.com*, June 7, 2022. www.history.com/news/us-overthrow-foreign-governments.

Mitchell, Taiyler S. "Dem Lawmakers Speak Out Against Cop City Arrests." *HuffPost*, June 5, 2023. www.huffpost.com/entry/lawmakers-cop-city-arrests-atlanta_n_647cf7a3e4b023 25c5e1608e.

"Native Knowledge 360°: The Removal of the Muscogee Nation." National Museum of the American Indian. Accessed 2023.

"NLG Condemns State Repression against Atlanta Solidarity Fund Activists." National Lawyers Guild, May 31, 2023. National Lawyers Guild.

"Public Safety Training Center." Atlanta Police Foundation. Accessed 2023. https://atlantapolicefoundation.org/programs/public-safety-training-center/.

Pulley, Brett, "Heirs to $35 Billion Fortune Face Off Over Atlanta's Controversial 'Cop City'," *Bloomberg*, May 10, 2024.

"OITNC" (*Organizing Is the New Cool*). FTP Movement documentary. www.organizingisthenewcool.com/about.

Open Secrets, Super Pacs. www.opensecrets.org/political-action-committees-pacs/super-pacs/2022.

Ossoff, Jon. Twitter post, June 4, 2023. https://twitter.com/ossoff/status/1665436838956347392.

Peisner, David, "Fergie Chambers is Heir to One of America's Richest Families — and Determined to See the U.S. Fall." *Rolling Stone*, March 24, 2024.

Radde, Kaitlyn. "Autopsy Reveals Anti-'Cop City' Activist's Hands Were Raised When Shot and Killed." *NPR*, March 11, 2023. www.npr.org/2023/03/11/1162843992/cop-city-atlanta-activist-autopsy.

Rico, R.J. "Atlanta Organizers Unveil Plan to Take 'Cop City' Fight to the Ballot Box." *PBS*, June 7, 2023. www.pbs.org/newshour/politics/atlanta-organizers-unveil-plan-to-take-cop-city-fight-to-the-ballot-box.

Rico, R.J. "Muddy Clothes? 'Cop City' Activists Question Police Evidence." *AP News*, March 24, 2023. https://apnews.com/article/cop-city-protest-domestic-terrorism-atlanta-6d114e109d489d316f588f51c7cab0cc.

Rico, R.J. "'Stop Cop City' Activists Pack Atlanta City Hall Ahead of Crucial Vote." *AP News*, June 6, 2023. https://apnews.com/article/cop-city-vote-atlanta-city-council-d782604c15874e441570654ea362e0ef.

Rico, R.J. "Atlanta Clerk Sued for Denying 'Stop Cop City' Petition Lets Effort Move Forward." *ABC News*, June 21, 2023. https://abcnews.go.com/US/wireStory/atlanta.

Roitman, Ariella. "Georgia State Police Return Home after Two-Week Israeli Training." *The Jerusalem Post*. JPost.com, July 22, 2022. www.jpost.com/israeli-news/article-711682.

Scott, Matt. "APD, Gbi Raid Bail Fund, Arrest Three Organizers." *Atlanta Community Press Collective*, June 12, 2023.

Seidman, Derek. "Corporate Backers of the Blue: How Corporations Bankroll U.S. Police Foundations." *Eyes on the Ties*, June 18, 2020. https://news.littlesis.org/2020/06/18/

corporate-backers-of-the-blue-how-corporations-bankroll-u-s-police-foundations/.

Shahshahani, Azadeh, and Collin P. Poirot. "The DOJ Is Using 'Foreign Agents' Accusations to Repress Black Liberation Organizers." *The Nation*, April 26, 2023. www.thenation.com/article/politics/foreign-agents-registration-act-political-repression/.

Shahtahmasebi, Darius, "West Papau: The Genocide That is Being Ignored by the World." *Indigenous Peoples Major Group for Sustainable Development*, nd.

Simon, Morgan. "Cops And Donuts Go Together More Than You Thought: The Corporations Funding Cop City in Atlanta." *Forbes*, March 14, 2023. www.forbes.com/sites/morgansimon/2023/03/14/cops-and-donuts-go-together-more-than-you-thought-the-corporations-funding-cop-city-in-atlanta/? sh=146c8f76bc60.

"16 Senior Police and Public Safety Executives Return from Police Executive Training in Israel." *Georgia State News Hub*, November 19, 2021. Andrew Young School of Policy Studies. https://news.gsu.edu/2021/11/19/16-senior-police-and-public-safety-executives-return-from-police-executive-training-in-israel/.

"16 Senior Police and Public Safety Executives Return from Police Executive Training in Israel Shot and Killed." *NPR*, March 11, 2023. www.npr.org/2023/03/11/1162843992/cop-city-atlanta-activist-autopsy.

Square Mile Media Atlanta. "55 TRINITY – 'I DON'T WANT COP CITY' Rev. Keyanna Jones." Youtube, 6:06. March 6, 2023. www.youtube.com/watch?v=tnFbsm3k2Oc.

"Statement from the Atlanta Solidarity Fund Regarding Attorney General's Investigation into Transactions, Donors." Document Cloud, June 2, 2023. Atlanta Solidarity Fund. www.documentcloud.org/documents/23833003-atlanta-solidarity-fund-investigation-response-statement-1-docx-1.

"Stop Cop City," Community Movement Builders. https://communitymovementbuilders.org/stop-cop-city/.

Tatum, Gloria. "Forest Defenders Reoccupy Weelaunee to Stop Cop City." *People's Tribune*, March 12, 2023. https://

peoplestribune.org/2023/03/forest-defenders-reoccupy-weelaunee-to-stop-cop-city/.

Tatum, Gloria. "Native Americans Share Concerns over Fate of Forest." *Streets of Atlanta*, May 3, 2022. https://streetsofatlanta.blog/2022/05/02/native-americans-share-concerns-over-fate-of-forest/.

Thigpen, Madeline, "How the Stop Cop City Movement Inspired Angela Davis." CAPITAL B Atlanta, April 14, 2023.

"21st Century Community Policing." Atlanta Police Foundation. Accessed 2023. https://atlantapolicefoundation.org/.

UNHRC, Report of the independent international commission of inquiry on the protests in the Occupied Palestinian Territory, 25 February–22 March 2019, online.

The United Fruit Company and the 1954 Guatemalan Coup, 2023. https://ufcguatemala.voices.wooster.edu/.

Valencia, Nick, Devon M. Sayers, and Pamela Kirkland. "Climate Activist Killed in 'Cop City' Protest Sustained 57 Gunshot Wounds, Official Autopsy Says, but Questions about Gunpowder Residue Remain." *CNN*, April 20, 2023. www.cnn.com/2023/04/20/us/cop-city-activist-killed-dekalb-county-medical-examiner/index.html.

Walter Rodney Foundation, https://twitter.com/RodneyProject/status/1642926791042924544, April 3, 2023.

Washington, DC: Department of the Navy, 1998.

Williams, Stanley Tookie, *Blue Rage, Black Redemption: A Memoir*, New York: Touchstone Books/Simon & Schuster, 2007.

Wolfe-Rocca, Ursula. "Why We Should Teach About the FBI's War on the Civil Rights Movement." Zinn Education Project, March 1, 2016. www.zinnedproject.org/if-we-knew-our-history/fbi-war-civil-rights-movement/.

Wright, Julia. "France's Racism Still on Display as It Denies Its Colonial Past – and Present." *Truthout*, July 12, 2023.

Youth Justice Project. "Projection: Spoken Word Performance by Hausson Byrd." YouTube video, 3:28. www.youtube.com/watch?v=XLptzN_zvBo.

Thanks to our Patreon subscriber:

Ciaran Kane

Who has shown generosity and comradeship in support of our publishing.

Check out the other perks you get by subscribing to our Patreon – visit patreon.com/plutopress.

Subscriptions start from £3 a month.

The Pluto Press Newsletter

Hello friend of Pluto!

Want to stay on top of the best radical books
we publish?

Then sign up to be the first to hear about our
new books, as well as special events,
podcasts and videos.

You'll also get 50% off your first order with us
when you sign up.

Come and join us!

Go to bit.ly/PlutoNewsletter